Diamonds Eternal

Diamonds Eternal

BY VICTOR ARGENZIO

David McKay Company, Inc.
New York

DIAMONDS ETERNAL

Copyright © 1974 by Victor Argenzio

All rights reserved, including the right to reproduce
this book, or parts thereof, in any form, except for
the inclusion of brief quotations in a review.

Library of Congress Catalog Card Number: 73-84072
Manufactured in the United States of America
ISBN: 0-679-50427-3

To Margaret

CONTENTS

In Grateful Acknowledgment   ix
Foreword   xi

Diamonds and the World

1   The World of Diamonds   3
2   The Eternal Diamond   13
3   The Greatest Diamonds of All Time   28
4   Jewels of History   60
5   The Queen's Necklace   78
6   The Light of Peace   86
7   Where Diamonds Come From   94
8   A Visit to Kimberley   116
9   Mining: The Search for Needles in a Haystack   130
10 The Diamond Cutters   141
11 From Mine to Milady   154
12 The Seamy Side of Diamonds   170
13 Diamonds U.S.A.   180
14 Synthetic Gem Diamonds   189
15 Offbeat   194
16 Diamonds at Work   200
17 Diamonds for Men   209
18 My Life with Diamonds: A Compilation of
    Reminiscences and Personal Observations   213

Diamonds and You

1   Buying a Diamond   227
2   The Meaning of "Carat"   230
3   How Clarity Affects Value   234
4   What Cut Does for the Diamond   239
5   Color and Its Importance   249
6   Some Important Questions and Answers
    About Diamonds   253

7	Diamonds as an Investment	259
8	A Word about Insurance	265
9	Care for Your Diamonds	267
	Glossary	269
	Bibliography	276
	Acknowledgments	281
	Index	283

In Grateful Acknowledgment

My deepest appreciation is extended to the many persons and firms without whose help this book could not have been written. In particular, I wish to thank:

—N. W. Ayer and Son, Inc., and its senior vice president, Robert Van Riper, whose staff has borne my inquiries with patience and provided me with invaluable assistance.

—DeBeers Consolidated Mines, Ltd., and Anglo American Corp., whose officials extended many courtesies that provided instructive and delightful experiences.

—My friend Bill Hosokawa, who managed somehow to find time from his extremely busy schedule to help me put my manuscript into readable form.

—My friend Gene Lindberg, who gave me so much time in explaining technical subjects which were beyond me.

—The Gemological Institute of America, from whose vast storehouse of material I have helped myself liberally.

—All the great publications which keep jewelers aware of what is happening in their profession. Particularly useful were the *Jewelers Circular-Keystone* and its news editor, Allen Ward who has given me invaluable assistance on technical matters; the *National Jeweler;* and *International Diamonds* and its editor, A. N. Wilson.

—My publishers, David McKay Company, Inc., and James Louttit, their administrative vice president, who treat me with the same courtesy and extend the same benefits of their great skills as they do their most popular authors.

—The men to whom I sent one or more chapters for review and comments:

Robert Van Riper of N. W. Ayer and Son, Inc., New York;

John Burls, Director, Industrial Diamond Information
Bureau, London;
Charles A. Schiffmann of Gübelin, Lucerne;
Peter Silveri of Peter Silveri and Associates, New
York;
Dr. Arthur M. Bueche, of General Electric Company,
Schenectady;
Richard Liddicoat, President of the Gemological Insti-
tute of America, Los Angeles.

—And last, but far from least, my wife, Margaret,
who was the source of encouragement when it was
needed (and this was frequently), who was always present when I traveled (I am unable now to travel without
assistance), who helped an inept writer keep his notes and
photographs where they could be found, and who even
went to bat helping with the typing when the need arose.
Thank you, wife and No. 1 helper.

Foreword

When I wrote *The Fascination of Diamonds* in 1966, it didn't occur to me that I would ever write another book on the same subject. I didn't realize then that the diamond world, like all others, is subject to constant change.

Who would have thought, a few years ago, science could succeed in making a synthetic gem diamond? I was so sure that this would never happen that I brashly asserted, on the second page of *Fascination*, that while man had split the atom, explored space, and created material as hard as the diamond, "he has not succeeded in duplicating its gemlike qualities." How I wish that this thought had not been expressed at the very outset of the book!

Then, who would have thought, only a decade ago, that the U.S.S.R. would become the world's second largest diamond-producing nation? Or *that tiny Israel would dislodge* Belgium as the world's largest cutters of diamonds after being a nation for only twenty-five years.

Many other changes have taken place in the diamond industry. Japan has become a major buyer of diamonds. Hong Kong, which has developed into a very important diamond-trading center, was the scene of one of the greatest diamond transactions of all time. In 1972, a jeweler in that British Crown Colony sold the great 125.65-carat Jonker Diamond, whose whereabouts had been unknown for years, to a Japanese businessman for $3,500,000. This is possibly the highest price ever paid for a single cut and fashioned diamond.

I was surprised and delighted to receive many hundreds of letters from readers of my book. I still get them—warm, friendly letters which have proved to me that diamonds are of real interest to people. When a British edition of *Fascination* was published, the letters that came to me convinced me that this feeling is world-wide.

So I have undertaken to write this second book on

diamonds. It contains a great deal of additional information, more stories about famous diamonds, and reports on recent developments in the industry. All in all, it is a much more complete and, I believe, a better volume.

It is my sincere wish that through this book my love for the world's greatest jewel may be conveyed to you, my readers. My entire business career has been with diamonds and jewelry, and now, after more than half a century of unforgettable association with them, they always will be a part of me.

Victor Argenzio
Denver, Colorado, 1973

PART I

Diamonds and the World

1
The World of Diamonds

There is a time when nothing, nothing but a diamond will do.
—Anon.

It was a cold, blustery, rainy day, but thousands of New Yorkers stood in a blocks-long queue outside Cartier's windows to get a glimpse of the $1,000,000 diamond Richard Burton had purchased for Elizabeth Taylor. In an era when even the sight of men walking on the surface of the moon hardly causes a ripple of interest, this incident dramatizes as nothing else the enduring fascination of diamonds.

Ever since they first came to light, diamonds have been prized and glamorized, fought over, cherished, cov-

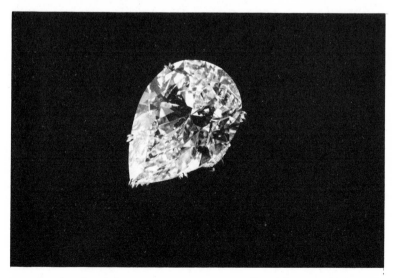

The Taylor–Burton diamond, actual size—a flawless pear-shape, 69.40-carat stone of exceptionally fine color and clarity. Credit: N. W. Ayer & Son, Inc.

eted, and even worshiped. What is there about this lump of carbon which so bewitched the ancients and continues to dazzle today's sophisticates? What is the diamond's magic power that puts starlight in the eyes of millions each year?

After more than half a century of buying and selling diamonds, I still do not have answers to these questions. I know only that I have observed at first hand the mysterious impact of this gem, and I never have ceased to marvel that any inanimate object could convey such warmth and meaning. I have looked into the souls of countless girls at the moment they first tried on an engagement ring. I believe that the full realization of the troth takes place for the first time when she sees the jewel on her finger.

In my early days as a salesman, I recall fearing greatly that the girl would not like the very large ring her fiancé wanted to buy for her. I needn't have worried. It was she who almost fainted in sheer delight when she put the ring on her finger.

An original creation by VanCleef & Arpels, Inc.

Diamonds are unique. They are nature's hardest substance, with beauty and brilliancy unmatched by any other jewel. Their rarity makes them precious and their origins add to their mystique.

They have been the cause of wars, murders, crime, despair, and suicides. Science and industry could not have attained their marvels without them. Untold thousands of refugees would have died without their help, and, above all, Cupid, the God of love, could not have performed his miracles without their magic.

Yet the diamond is only carbon, which comes in only one other form, graphite, which gives us lubricants, pencil leads, and other useful tools. Due to an inexplicable whim of nature, one is hard and precious, the other, soft and common. The difference is in their atomic structure.

The carbon atoms in graphite lie loosely in sheets that slide easily over each other. The same atoms in diamonds, however, are stacked tightly in an orderly manner and compressed into crystalline form by the enormous forces of nature. This explains why diamonds may be polished to a luster unequaled by any other gems. They are the most sought after of all jewels, so much so that millions of dollars are spent each year to purchase imitations which fulfill partially the yearning of many for the genuine.

How did the diamond get its name? Etymologists lean to the Greek "adamas," which means "invincible." "Diamond shape" as we know it on playing cards most likely came from a common shape in which diamonds frequently are found, the octahedron, which resembles two pyramids fused at their bases.

Diamonds are found in several parts of the world, with South Africa producing the greatest percentage, which it has for almost 100 years. Soviet Russia, now has attained second place, due to deposits discovered in Siberia.

Are diamonds found in the United States? Yes, some have been found in several states, probably picked up elsewhere by glaciers and deposited during the Ice Age. The only known authentic Kimberlite field—the "mother lode" of diamonds, so to speak—in all North America is in Pike County, Arkansas. Several good-sized gem diamonds—and thousands of small ones—have been recovered near the town of Murfreesboro.

The United States is the best customer for diamonds, consuming approximately fifty percent of the total world production. The more than 2,000,000 annual marriages in our country are responsible for the greatest part. A recent survey found that, of the eighty-seven percent of all American girls receiving engagement rings, ninety-seven percent of those chose a diamond. The preference for diamonds to bind a troth remains constant.

At one time, Americans purchased a larger percentage of the world's diamond production, but in the past few years Europe and Japan, which have accepted the diamond engagement custom, are increasing their share. The Japanese also are buying about twenty percent of the world's production of polished diamonds, mostly of the highest quality, for investment. Since Hong Kong is also becoming a major diamond distribution center, the Far East is second only to the United States as the largest single consumer of cut gems.

An exquisite diamond ring, an International Award Winner. Credit: Granat Bros., San Francisco

Diamonds sold in the United States exceed a whopping $500,000,000 annually. Among those with means, there is still a competitive wish to own large and beautiful diamonds, something which has persisted through the centuries. And Paolo Bulgari, the world-famous Roman jeweler, says: "People everywhere are eager for status symbols. With furniture and paintings, one looks at them

A variety of diamonds for a man, an International Award Winner. Credit: Gübelin, Lucerne

and enjoys them, but with jewelry, one wears it, owns it bodily. It is the most sophisticated status symbol wherever you go."

However, the great majority of diamonds sold are not showpieces. They are the smaller diamonds, equally cherished and every bit as proudly worn. The average price for individual gemstones is approximated at $350, with the size of the center diamond about .38 carat.

A recent jeweler's survey indicates that the man usually is accompanied by his fiancée when buying the engagement ring, that more than seventy percent of these buyers are in their twenties, and that they are sharper about their purchases than their predecessors, asking the right questions about the various qualities of the stone. More showed interest in color than in weight, cut, or internal quality, which shows good judgment. The survey also showed that it takes from ten minutes to an hour for the majority of engagement ring sales; fewer than three percent take over an hour, and five percent of sales are made in less than ten minutes.

My own experience has been that the purchase of a diamond is one of the most glamorous and thrilling events ever for youngsters contemplating marriage. Only the purchase of their first home compares to it, and most couples are not averse to prolonging the transaction. It's when the couple brings in family or outside "experts" that the scene often becomes less than tranquil.

Diamonds, while they are the hardest known substance, may be chipped or damaged if struck just right against a hard object or if dropped on a hard surface. Like any other precious object, diamonds should be treated with care. Like wood, the diamond has a grain, and, if struck along this grain, damage can follow. This doesn't happen often, but it does occur, as any insurance company can attest.

Indeed, many years ago following an article published by *Consumer's Research* Magazine, I received more comment on this fact than anything else I had mentioned. A number of readers said that when their diamonds chipped they had thought that imitations had been sold to them.

Although diamonds have a high unit value, they are measured by weight—like meat or vegetables. However, weight is only one of several factors involved in determining their value. The basic unit is a carat, a word derived

The basic diamond measure is the carat, a word derived from "carob," a small Oriental bean which was remarkably uniform in size.

from carob, a small Oriental bean, not unlike a coffee bean in size. The carob seeds are remarkable for their uniformity of size, and they were used in ancient times in weighing gems. A carat is 1/142 of an avoirdupois ounce, or 200 milligrams. A well-cut and proportioned round diamond of one carat measures almost exactly 1/4 inch in diameter. However, because factors other than weight are involved in determining the value of a diamond, a 1-carat stone could be worth as little as $100 or over $5000.

The largest diamond ever found, the Cullinan, weighed in its original state an unbelievable 3106 carats —or 1⅓ pounds avoirdupois, which gives us a more realistic idea of its weight. It was as large as a good-sized man's fist. When the Cullinan was cut, it yielded the world's largest finished stone, the second largest diamond extant, and, as if this weren't enough, several other gems.

The smallest diamonds are tiny indeed. After cutting, they may weigh less than a single point, which is one hundredth of a carat. Few pieces of jewelry use such tiny sets, but an Italian craftsman, Luigi Stumpo, succeeded after years of research in setting what are probably the smallest diamonds ever used, in the hands of watches. Six stones, each measuring only 0.7 of a millimeter in diameter, were set in the minute hand, and five in the second hand, in a line of Audemars Piguet watches. Thomas Edison used diamond points in his earliest talking machines.

Eighty percent of diamond yield is too poor to classify as gem quality. These are used in industry and science, where their hardness makes them invaluable. A 19-carat industrial diamond was once used in an American au-

Statue of an Egyptian king, 1400–1300 B.C., *from the National Cairo Museum, with a wooden tray of diamonds. Credit: Fine Jewelers' Guild*

tomobile factory. For sixteen years this stone performed, receiving such hard wear that it had been worn down to less than a quarter of a carat. Too small for further service, the stone was ground into dust for grinding and polishing other diamonds, and its useful life prolonged.

Diamonds helped create the marvelously precise machines that took man to the moon; and, in answer to the obvious question, so far there has been no indication of any diamonds in rocks returned from that planet.

Gem diamonds are used for many purposes other than engagement rings and jewelry. They are employed to advertise products, to call attention to major promotional events, to commemorate anniversaries, and in dozens of other roles where a special elegance is desired. They have been used in such disparate ways as the adornment of an Oriental belly dancer's navel, to the recent purchase of a huge diamond—one of the largest found in years—for the sole purpose of being displayed with the proceeds to be used to promote peace in the world. Aptly, this magnificent gem has been named "Light of Peace." I will have more to say about it later.

The way diamonds are distributed, from mine to consumer, is a story in itself. The rough stones are sold in London to a few scores of cutters and wholesalers. Thence they go to cutting factories and then to the bourses and exchanges (called "clubs") of the world.

In New York, the hub of America's diamond business, ninety percent of the diamonds go through the hands of hundreds of dealers located mostly on 47th Street between Fifth and Sixth avenues. This is aptly called Diamond Street. The major dealers have offices upstairs in closely guarded rooms, but many small dealers do business out of their pockets in the streets.

Wholesale dealers have their own private world and ethics. Over the years they have developed a tight fraternity founded on mutual respect and implicit trust. Although they deal in huge sums, their dealings with each other are casual. A deal may be sealed with a handshake and an old Hebrew expression, *"Mazel und broche,"* meaning "Good luck and blessings." Used by Jews and non-Jews alike, this is as binding as any written contract, and all agreements are scrupulously observed.

There is never a lack of stories about Diamond Street. A woman walks out of one of the retail shops admiring a very large diamond ring she has just purchased. It slips off her finger and vanishes down a sewer, to be recovered after much excitement and anguish. An alarm accidentally triggered brings out a dozen squad cars which block off both ends of the street. In a small restaurant, two dealers haggle over a loose stone which is inadvertently flipped into a bowl of hot soup. The diamond is recovered, the soup wiped off, and the transaction brought to a conclusion. Robberies and thefts occur, even under the eyes of plainclothesmen and police on what probably is the best-patrolled street in the world.

Newspapers occasionally carry stories about the disposition of the diamond ring after an engagement is broken. A precedent of sorts was established in 1947 when a disillusioned suitor asked a Los Angeles court for the return of a $2000 ring after the girl broke the engagement. Since there seemed to be nothing in California law which applied, the judge found that under ancient Roman law, going back 2000 years, the engagement ring was not considered the woman's property until the marriage took place.

The Romans held that an engagement ring was a symbol of troth, and if the troth was broken the ring reverted to the donor. The plaintiff was awarded the ring, but the woman was allowed to keep other jewelry he had given her.

In Paris, a judge ruled that the man does not have the right to take the ring back unless it is the woman who breaks the engagement, which was not the case in this instance. "But the ring was expensive," complained the man, who with Gallic fervor had broken his fiancée's finger while retrieving the ring during a quarrel. His Honor fined the man $40 for the broken finger and returned the ring to her "for proper wearing as soon as the finger mended." Could King Solomon have done better?

2
The Eternal Diamond

The evil eye shall have no power to harm
Him that shall wear the diamond as a charm.
—Anon. Roman poet, 2nd Century A. D.

Just as we do not know how diamonds were created by nature, so their early history is shrouded in mystery. From earliest times, they were greatly valued and held in the highest esteem. We don't know why; certainly they weren't beautiful because cutting and faceting were totally unknown. Perhaps it was the diamond's hardness which so intrigued the ancients, with the hardness carrying a mystic symbolism. Whatever the reason, diamonds were eagerly sought. Because kings and emperors held the power, they were the ones who gathered diamonds into their treasuries and used them in one fashion or another.

In the first century A. D., the Roman philosopher and historian Pliny the Elder noted that diamonds were hard, rare, and valuable, and he wrote that only kings and emperors wore them. He probably was among the first to start some of the many fables about diamonds. The wearer of a diamond, Pliny wrote, had a magic charm of protection when in battle; swallowing a diamond surely would neutralize poison, and diamonds were certain talismans against insanity. Then he unwittingly caused the destruction of many diamonds by asserting that the best way to check their genuineness was to place them on an anvil and smite them with a hammer! How many were destroyed in this manner is left to the imagination.

Little is known about the early wearers of diamonds aside from unnamed kings and emperors. One of the first mentioned is Zenobia, Queen of Palmyra, about A. D. 270. It seems that she had a "dazzling" diamond clasp at the

13

shoulder, so valuable that a province could have been added to her kingdom if she had preferred it in place of the jewelry.

Although diamonds couldn't have "dazzled" in 270—the science of cutting, polishing, and faceting wasn't developed until many centuries later—they were sometimes so described. Could the ancients have divined their eventual potential and beauty?

An admirer of diamonds—Charlemagne, King of the Franks in A.D. *768. Credit: B. T. Batsford, Ltd.*

Charlemagne, who was made king of the Franks in A. D. 768, admired and wore diamonds. He and his immediate successors took great interest in learning and culture and were instrumental in lifting the veil of the Dark Ages. Charlemagne forbade the custom of burying jewels with the dead. Apparently he felt diamonds should be worn and enjoyed and not, like their late owners, be laid to rest.

Marco Polo, the great Venetian traveller, in his celebrated trips to the East in the thirteenth century, was cordially received in the court of the Mongol emperor Kublai Khan. He returned with fabulous stories of wealth, describing mounds of diamonds and other jewels. These were probably part of the booty gathered by Kublai's famous and notorious grandfather, Genghis Khan. As we know, Marco's stories, while true, were so fantastic that they weren't believed when he returned to Venice.

Incredible, also, are the stories of the sixteenth- and seventeenth-century Moguls of India. Although they had been plundered of much of their treasures during the centuries, so that diamonds which originated in their country became scattered, they still had untold quantities of them.

A rare inventory made by Mogul Emperor Jehangir mentions eighty pounds of uncut diamonds! Considering that a single ounce calls for 142 carats, Jehangir gives us some guide to the riches which were in the hands of those emperors. Also listed in the inventory were seven thrones studded with diamonds, pearls, and other precious stones, and a bathtub described as seven by five feet and decorated elaborately with diamonds "to relieve the monotony and drabness of gold!"

Emperor Jehangir's son, Shah Jehan, the fifth Mogul emperor and builder of the Taj Mahal, was reputed to have a better knowledge of diamond values than any jeweler in the East. Moreover, he had first choice of the then richest diamond mines in the world, India's famous Golconda fields. Only stones he rejected were allowed to be sold to others.

Jean Baptiste Tavernier, born in Paris in the seven-

Shah Jehan, who built the Taj Mahal, had first choice of the gems from the world's richest mines, India's famous Golconda fields. Credit: N. W. Ayer & Son, Inc.

Jean Baptiste Tavernier, a merchant of precious stones in the seventeenth century. Credit: N. W. Ayer & Son, Inc.

teenth century, was the Marco Polo of his time. A merchant of precious stones, he made six trips to Turkey, Persia, and India, which took the better part of his long life. The European world was indebted to him, as we all are today, for the knowledge of diamonds he amassed and brought back with him. Certainly he understood the importance of weights, imperfections, and colors of diamonds.

When Tavernier visited Shah Jehan's son, Aurangzeb, he was shown some of the world's greatest diamonds. Never had he beheld such wealth. His description of the Peacock Throne of the Moguls bears repetition. Adorned with hundreds of diamonds, emeralds, pearls, and rubies, its feature was one large diamond close to 100 carats, possibly the size of an American half-dollar piece, which had been set so the emperor could admire it when seated. Near the throne were canopies studded with gems.

The Peacock Throne of the Moguls was adorned with hundreds of diamonds, emeralds, pearls, and rubies, and featured one large diamond of almost 100 carats. Credit: Topkapi Museum

The throne took its name from two peacocks carved across the back, their spread tails inlaid with pearls, rubies, and emeralds and topped by a "sun" of dazzling diamonds. The throne now stands in Gulistan Palace in Teheran, Iran, formerly known as Persia. Nadir Shah,

The Peacock dais of Persia, topped by a "sun" of dazzling diamonds. Credit: National Bank of Teheran, Iran

who conquered large sections of India in 1739, is believed to have brought the throne back from Delhi. As experienced as Tavernier was, he said that viewing the Mogul treasure was the thrill of his life.

Tavernier purchased a large number of gems to take back to Europe. Among them was a great blue diamond which, it is generally believed, was recut and became the Hope Diamond. Some writers have it that the Shah didn't want to dispose of the blue stone and that the doughty Tavernier stole it. The truth will never be known, but it all adds to the mystique of diamond lore.

Among Tavernier's royal clients was Louis XIV of France, who bought thousands of carats of diamonds from him. Louis was so pleased that he showered gold, lands, and the title of "Baron" on his compatriot. It was Louis

XVI who flaunted his diamonds more lavishly than any of
his predecessors, showering them on his queen, Marie
Antoinette.

Napoleon I, likewise, loved diamonds and he collected them on his campaigns. After Empress Marie
Louise gave him the son that Josephine failed to provide,
Napoleon showered her with diamond jewelry including a
necklace in the form of a circle of twenty-eight large round
diamonds. Suspended about the necklace are other large
stones, whose total weight is 275 carats. It is one of the
most famous jewels of historic as well as intrinsic value.
After Marie Louise's death, it was passed down through
successive generations and then ultimately into other
hands. In 1962, Mrs. Herbert May of Washington, D. C.,
who owned it at that time, presented it to the Smithsonian
Institution.

A dazzling gift from Napoleon to his empress, Marie Louise, a circle of twenty-
eight large round diamonds. Credit: Smithsonian Institution

The Empress Josephine's tiara. This famous tiara was made for the Empress Josephine. Ordered by Napoleon, it was designed and executed by the French jewelers VanCleef & Arpels. Credit: VanCleef & Arpels, Inc.

A commoner in the French court of Charles VII made news in 1444 as the first woman, not a queen or empress, to wear diamonds. Agnès Sorel was her name, and she became an instant celebrity. The story has been told and retold.

Agnès hoped to become Charles' favorite and decided on an approach that would make an unforgettable impression. Borrowing some good-sized diamonds, she had them mounted into a showy necklace which she wore to the court one night. Since this was some years before lapidaries learned the secret of symmetrical faceting to bring out the gems' true beauty, one may be forgiven for suspecting that Agnès made a bold play to accent her not inconsiderable charms revealed by the low-cut gowns in vogue at the time. It has been said that the eyes of the good king almost left their sockets when he gazed on her.

But the noblest function of the diamond, and its real

raison d'être is the part it has played as the symbol of love and token of betrothal. This custom dates as far back as 1477, when Maximilian I, Holy Roman Emperor, sealed his troth with a diamond. He started a custom which has

Diamonds have been a symbol of love and a token of bethrothal since Maximilian I, Holy Roman Emperor, sealed his troth with a diamond in the fifteenth century.

grown almost universal. Mary of Burgundy accepted the diamond joyfully, and a profitable marriage ensued, bringing new lands under Maximilian's rule.

Understandably, diamonds played a large part in the romantic fiction of Europe. The greatest writers of the time must have succumbed to the fascination of diamonds because they became the subject of many novels, as indeed they are now. In our century, stories about diamonds still make good reading. A true story with all the romance of fiction came to light in the *International Diamond Annual*.

It starts in 1927, when a South African digger named Houthaker found a large, blackish diamond which weighed 33 carats. He sold it to a dealer, but retained a half interest in it. The purchaser showed it to several persons, including the late Sir Ernest Oppenheimer, former chairman of De Beers Consolidated Diamond Mines, Ltd. Sir Ernest thought it just an unusual piece of bort (industrial-quality diamond) but advised him to send it to the Goudvis Company of Amsterdam, who were, in turn, buyers for the well-known firm of D. Drukker of Amsterdam.

The five Goudvis brothers looked it over and called in others, including the master cutter, to view the stone. Everyone labeled it a piece of ordinary bort and all wondered why Sir Ernest had ever advised having it sent to them.

All, that is, except the eldest Goudvis brother. Holding the stone under a strong lamp, he insisted that he could perceive a faint light in the diamond. On his insistence, they cabled Houthaker for permission to polish a "window" on each side to permit better viewing of the interior. Two carats of diamond were ground away, but the stone remained black.

Again, contrary to the opinion of all, the elder brother declared firmly, "I see light." More cables were sent back and forth, and it was decided to make more windows. After losing 10 carats, almost a third of the stone's weight, the diamond now took on a brownish look. Then the master cutter, who was doing the work, also saw a faint beam of light.

He removed the stone from the wheel and hurried to the eldest Goudvis. Under a strong lamp, a reddish gleam was now visible. Excitement mounted, as diamonds which give out reddish gleams aren't encountered every day.

Then there were heated discussions as to the shape best suited for the stone. Months of study, plus further polishing, finally produced an emerald cut–shaped diamond which weighed 5.05 carats. It was of finest internal quality and, miraculously, red in color. Examined by candlelight in a totally darkened room, "it was as if a drop of blood had fallen on the hand that held the diamond."

No one had any idea of its value. No diamond dealer

in Amsterdam would hazard a guess. They all knew that a flawless stone of that size in finest color was rare enough, but a red diamond answering this description was without precedent.

The stone was taken to New York and shown to four foremost jewelers. None was interested in its purchase, so the youngest Goudvis brother, who had been entrusted with the task, returned to Amsterdam. Then one day a cable from Tiffany's brought the message that they had a buyer.

Again the young man made the long journey (it's quicker these days) to New York. Tiffany's client offered $100,000. The eldest Goudvis wanted to sell. The others, knowing they had something unique, held out for $150,000. The customer lost interest—and back went the diamond into the safe at home.

Then came the Great Depression, followed by World War II and then the Nazi occupation of Holland. Many conflicting tales of what happened to the valuable red diamond were circulated. In the meantime, the five Goudvis brothers died, and with them disappeared all knowledge of what became of their beautiful red diamond. Like so many great diamonds, this one has disappeared, possibly for all time.

The weighing ceremony of the Aga Khan in 1946 was as outlandish as a tale out of the Arabian Nights. In observance of his seventy-fifth birthday, a diamond jubilee was celebrated in Bombay, India, and Dar es Salaam in Tanganyika, now Tanzania. The value of the Aga Khan's weight in diamonds was to be contributed to his favorite charities by the wealthy members of the Moslem sect of which he was spiritual leader.

While richly adorned princes, rajahs, and sultans crowded about him, he deposited his bulky 243 pounds in a swivel chair which had been placed on a huge scale. Case after case of diamonds—549,824 carats in all—were needed to counterbalance his weight. The diamonds, which were loaned for the occasion by the London diamond group, were of industrial quality so that a com-

The Aga Khan celebrated his seventy-fifth birthday in 1946 with a gift of his weight in diamonds. He weighed a hefty 243 pounds. Credit: World Wide Photos

paratively low value per carat could be obtained. Even so, the value of his weight in diamonds was reported at $1,500,000. The Aga Khan's followers subsequently contributed this amount in gold, cash, and gems, and this tidy fortune was duly turned over to worthy causes. In the second weighing in Tanganyika, Aga Khan was found to have lost half a pound. That half pound deprived his charities of $3500.

Diamonds rarely lend themselves to humor, but once in a while there are funny stories about them. One day during the Depression, Harpo Marx, the comedian, went into Tiffany's to look at loose diamonds. He did not identify himself. He acted very furtively and Tiffany guards were alerted. Finally he started for the door and broke into a run with two guards at his heels. Harpo fell. As he did, scores of loose stones came out of his pockets and scattered over the street. He was collared by the guards and returned to the store while others scrambled frantically to retrieve the stones. Of course they turned out to be five-and-dime variety and Harpo won a wager with a friend who had dared him to pull off the trick.

Diamond Jim Brady, the flamboyant playboy of the nineties—the one who had Tiffany's make a solid gold

Diamond Jim Brady, right, *presented Lillian Russell with a diamond-studded bicycle. Credit: World Wide Photos*

chamber pot with an eye painted at the bottom as a gift for Lillian Russell—had diamonds set profusely in a bicycle for her. It also is said that he had some set in her garters.

While diamonds occasionally tend to bring out the bizarre in some, jewelers often are asked to make special, quite touching personal pieces to convey sentiments of love and tenderness. Two of my favorite stories, both from personal experience, follow.

One young man, newly engaged, asked me to suggest something for his fiancée's birthday. She was enjoying her diamond ring so much, he said, that he wanted to use a diamond for his gift. He shyly suggested a tiny gold cage which could be worn on a chain, with a revolving disk inside set with a small diamond; and under the diamond, on both sides, he wanted engraved the words, "I am loved," so tiny that only she could see it. There wasn't much money involved, but I was delighted to carry out the commission because it gave me renewed faith in human nature.

And I shall never forget an incident which happened shortly after we opened our jewelry store and when I was at a most impressionable age.

A newly married couple who had bought their rings from me came in one day to make a small purchase. While it was being wrapped, the bride spied a lovely diamond necklace in the showcase and asked its price. It was $450, far more than her husband could afford at the time. She tried it on, took it to a mirror, and her desire for it was very obvious. As they left the store she turned back to give the necklace one more long and wistful look.

The husband had been watching her intently and secretly signaled to me to hold it out. Later that day he telephoned to say he wanted to present it to her for her birthday, which was several months away. He said he didn't earn enough to afford the piece, but he would try to arrange something, and would I hold it out for the period. Of course I agreed and took it out of stock.

A month later, I received a cashier's check from him for $100. Four weeks after that I received another cashier's draft for the same amount. I surmised that he was earning extra money and didn't want the transactions shown on their joint bank account.

A few days later, the girl came in to "have my watch checked," but it was obvious she wanted another look at the necklace. Well, of course, it wasn't there, and she almost broke into tears. But she pulled herself together and said to me, "It was so beautiful, and how I would love to have had it, but of course we couldn't buy anything like that."

As she walked out the door I couldn't help thinking again, as I had done so many times before, that I was in a business which gave pleasure. I could just picture her happiness and the pride of the husband as he presented it to her on her birthday.

But this wasn't the end of the story.

The third check arrived; then the fourth, leaving a balance of just $50 and the birthday just a few weeks off. And then the ceiling fell in. I got the details of what happened later. It seems the husband had taken a night job to make the extra money, but had told his wife that he was taking a special course at his regular place of work.

Unfortunately, one of his wife's friends happened to see him outside the place where he was moonlighting. What's more, he was talking to a woman who was also employed at the same place. I suppose it was inevitable the friend would call the young wife and ask what her husband was doing out at night with a pretty young lady.

Happily, everything turned out well—except that the birthday gift wasn't a surprise anymore.

3
The Greatest Diamonds of All Time

The diamond is beyond contradiction the most beautiful creation in the hands of God in the order of inanimate things.
— Memoirs of the Marquise de Montespan, mistress of Louis XIV

The great diamonds of the world have exciting and amazing histories which add to the endless fascination of these incomparable gems, a fascination that grows with the years.

There are scores of gems which fall into the "greatest diamond" category, but I have included in this chapter only those that have interested me most through the years. Among them are the most famous diamond in the United States, the greatest of the British Crown Jewels, the pride of the diamond collection of the Kremlin, the chief diamond attraction of the Topkapi Royal Museum in Istanbul, and the main diamond of Iran and that of the Louvre. They are all proudly displayed and attract millions of viewers annually.

THE HOPE

The most famous gem in the United States is the Hope Diamond, often ranked as second only to the Kohinoor in world fame. It is the largest blue diamond in existence. The great French gem expert Jean Baptiste Tavernier first heard about this blue diamond in 1642 on one of his trips to India. After much inquiry, he found it mounted in the eye, or perhaps it was the forehead, of the statue of the god Rama Sita. It is not known for certain how Tavernier acquired it. He may have purchased it. But

The most famous gem in the United States, the Hope Diamond is the largest blue diamond in existence. Credit: N. W. Ayer & Son, Inc.

some historians say the guardian priests refused to sell it, so Tavernier pried the diamond from the statue and fled.

What is known for certain is that he appeared at the court of Louis XIV of France in 1668 with the blue stone along with hundred of others. The blue diamond weighed

112.50 carats at the time. The King's expert, Sieur Pitau, cut the stone down to 62.50 carats in an attempt to improve its brilliance, and it became the principal jewel of the French Crown Jewel collection. It was named the Blue Diamond of the Crown.

When the French Revolution broke out in 1792, many of the crown jewels, including the Blue Diamond, were stolen from the Garde Meuble. While many of the jewels were recovered, the Blue Diamond was never found. It was traced to a diamond cutter in Holland who was reputed to have changed its shape so the French government couldn't lay claim to it, but there the trail vanished.

Then in 1830 a remarkable blue diamond, weighing 44.50 carats, appeared in London. No other blue diamond that large had ever been seen since Tavernier. It is now well authenticated that this stone had been recut from the Blue Diamond of the Crown, although it is impossible to say where it had been concealed for thirty-eight years.

The blue diamond was quickly purchased by Henry Philip Hope, a wealthy Londoner, in the same year. He died in 1839 and the stone passed on to his nephew, Sir Henry Thomas Hope, a banker. By this time the stone was well known as the Hope Diamond. When the widow of Henry Thomas died in 1887, she left the diamond to a grandson on condition that he adopt the Hope name.

The young lord's full name became Henry Francis Hope Pelham-Clinton-Hope, and he got the diamond. Eventually Lord Hope had to dispose of the diamond in partial liquidation of his debts, and it changed hands several times before Turkish Sultan Abdul Hamid II, who also owned the Idol's Eye, acquired it in 1908.

When he was deposed, the stone reached Paris by a round about route and was sold to French jeweler Pierre Cartier, who in turn sold it in 1911 to Mr. and Mrs. Edward B. McLean. McLean's wife, Evalyn Walsh McLean, a Colorado native, inherited a mining fortune which originated at Camp Bird Mine in southwestern Colorado. Mrs. McLean was intrigued by the diamond for the entire thirty-five years she owned it. She wore it often, displayed it, let her friends handle it. Jean Dickenson, in her *Book of Diamonds*, reports that at one time Mrs. McLean pawned the jewel to raise money to help ransom the kidnaped Lindbergh baby.

At her death in 1947, the McLean jewel collection was purchased by Harry Winston, noted New York jeweler. He presented the Hope Diamond to the Smithsonian Institution in Washington, where some 3,000,000 people view it annually. My wife and I once attended a small function in the Smithsonian's Gem Room and had a rare opportunity to view the Hope Diamond leisurely.

It is steel blue, the color accentuated by its circlet and necklace of diamonds of different cut which are all white. The necklace is in a shatter-proof glass case on the wall and makes a tremendous visual impression on the onlooker. But I was thinking of the tales which have accompanied the stone for a great part of its history. These tales, I decided, are the chief reason for its magnetism and why it is the principal attraction in the Gem Room. The Hope Diamond has been associated with bad luck. And, while most of us may laugh at superstitions, let us review some of the incidents which led to its reputation.

The legend of its evil influence was already in existence when Louis XIV purchased it. One of his mistresses refused to have anything to do with it but finally was persuaded to wear it. Almost immediately she lost her place as a favorite and was banished from the Court.

The stone passed on to Louis XVI. He and his wife, Marie Antoinette, received the guillotine treatment.

The Dutch cutter who changed its appearance had the stone stolen from him by his own son, who later killed himself—or was killed.

Lord Hope, the one who changed his name, died a bankrupt—after his wife ran off with another man.

Turkish Sultan Abdul Hamid II lost his throne and had to abdicate shortly after he acquired the stone in 1908.

After the McLeans acquired the stone, the bad luck associated with it struck and struck again. Her first son was killed in an auto crash. Her husband, implicated in the Teapot Dome scandal, died in a mental institution. When the stone was pawned to aid in the search for the Lindbergh baby, she was in contact with the imposter named Gaston Means. Her daughter died of an overdose of sleeping pills.

When Harry Winston, no believer in superstitions, bought the diamond together with the jewelry from the estate of Mrs. McLean in 1947 for $1,000,000, several stories appeared. The best is one which appeared in the *International Diamond Annual* in 1971. Let Harry tell his story here:

"A little later I was in Lisbon with my wife Edna. As our two sons were still quite young, Edna and I decided to return home on separate planes, as people with children often do. So Edna took off for New York on schedule on the Friday evening and I booked to follow the next day.

"Edna's plane landed in Santa Maria in the Azores for the usual refueling. Some slight engine trouble was discovered and there was a delay of some hours. The passengers chatted amongst themselves and it soon got around the lounge that Mrs. Harry Winston was a passenger. One man refused to continue the journey and asked to be booked on the next plane.

"On my way to the airport the next evening, I was handed a cablegram from Edna announcing her safe arrival. I put it in my pocket. On the plane I took a sedative and had a pleasant nap, with nobody in the adjoining seat to disturb me. On reboarding the plane at Santa Maria, after refueling, I found a very talkative man in the seat next to me. He told me how he had escaped from traveling on the same plane as the wife of the owner of the Hope Diamond. 'I'm not superstitious,' he claimed, 'but why should I tempt fate? I decided to change planes and here I am. Besides, there was engine trouble on that plane.

"He talked and talked for quite some time, but eventually grew quiet enough for me to begin to drop off to sleep again. Then his voice broke through to me: 'I wonder if that plane arrived safely.

"I could not resist it. I fished the cable out of my

pocket and passed it across to him to read. Then he gazed dumbly at me. He never opened his mouth again that night. I slept well."

An amusing incident was related by Dr. George Switzer, Curator of Minerals at the Smithsonian, in the December 1971 *National Geographic.*

The Hope Diamond was to be shown at the Louvre in Paris, and Dr. Switzer was to deliver it personally. En route, however, his plane landed so roughly in Philadelphia that the flight was canceled. The only other transatlantic flight available was to Frankfurt, West Germany, and, because he was anxious to deliver the gem, he took it. There was a long delay in Frankfurt, but he finally arrived in Paris.

A relieved committee of museum officials met him. They drove into the city—straight into an automobile accident. It wasn't serious, and the famous stone was shown and finally got safely back to its home at the Smithsonian, which, Dr. Switzer asserts, is not a bit unlucky to have it.

THE KOHINOOR

Perhaps the most famous and notorious diamond of all time is the Kohinoor. It has the longest recorded history, has been the cause of more intrigue and bloodshed, than any other gem. Several books have been written about it.

Early in its history, it was associated with power: He who owned the Kohinoor could rule the world. Gem historians have traced the Kohinoor back to 1304, when it was owned by the Rajah of Malwa, one of the Indian states south of Delhi. Undoubtedly, it was found centuries before that time.

The Sultan Baber, first of the Mogul emperors, came into possession of the Kohinoor in 1526. In his memoirs, Baber wrote that he received a quantity of precious stones, including the Kohinoor, after his son, Humayun, defeated the Rajah of Gwalior in a great battle. Baber says in his history that the diamond was so valuable that it "could

The Kohinoor diamond–replicas before and after refashioning. Credit: N. W. Ayer & Son, Inc.

pay half the expenses of the world." It weighed, then, 186 carats.

After Baber's death, the gems were passed down to each reigning Mogul, among them Shah Jehan, who, as I have said, built the Taj Mahal in memory of his beloved wife, Mumtaz Mahal. The gems remained in the hands of the Moguls until India, then ruled by Mohammed Shah, was invaded in 1739 by the Persians under Nadir Shah, leader of one of the most barbarous armies of all time. Nadir Shah seized the entire Mogul collection of jewels; but the Kohinoor, the gem he wanted most of all, was nowhere to be found. For two months he ransacked Delhi in search of the stone, ordering his men to pillage and burn until it was found.

When terror failed to produce the Kohinoor, Nadir Shah resorted to strategy. He questioned one of the favorites in the harem of Mohammed Shah and in some manner got the story out of her that the Shah always had it concealed in his turban, without which he never appeared in public.

Nadir Shah easily could have killed the Mogul and taken the diamond. It isn't clear why he didn't or why he hadn't already done so. Nonetheless, Nadir invited Mohammed Shah to an elaborately staged ceremony at which he reinstated the Mogul Sultan and vowed eternal friendship. At this point, Nadir Shah asked the Mogul to exchange turbans as a binding gesture. Mohammed Shah could not refuse. He gave up his turban—and the jewel—with no change of expression.

It is said that when Nadir Shah withdrew to his tent, he feverishly undid the turban, and there it was! The brilliance and beauty of the coveted stone was greater than he expected, and he exclaimed *"Kuh-i-noor,"* meaning "mountain of light" in Persian. The stone was shaped to resemble a small mountain. The gem was thus permanently named.

Violence swirled about the Kohinoor for the next several centuries. Nadir Shah's end was assassination, after which the stone passed to his son, Shah Rukh, an inept ruler who loved the Kohinoor so greatly that he would stare at it by the hour. When he was about to be deposed, he hid the diamond. He was horribly tortured to reveal the location of the stone but did not reveal the secret to his inquisitors.

The diamond passed from ruler to ruler, sometimes

through inheritance, sometimes through force. Ahmed Shah, his son Timur, Timur's son Zeman, and Zeman's brother Shah Shuja owned the stone for varying periods.

The Kohinoor as it was when used as an armlet. Credit: Gemological Institute of America

Shuja was exiled along with Zeman, and both fled to the court of Ranjit Singh, the so-called Lion of the Punjab, taking the Kohinoor with them. Ranjit Singh forced the brothers to give up the stone to him in return for sanctuary. He wore it in a bracelet for several years, cutting four grooves in it for the setting, and then had it reset in an armlet. After Ranjit Singh died, the Kohinoor remained for a century in the treasury of the Punjab of Lahore.

In 1849, a mutiny of the Sikh regiments led to the annexation of the Punjab to the British Empire, and the diamond was seized by the East India Company as partial indemnity. The following year it was presented to Queen Victoria to commemorate the 250th anniversary of the chartering of the East India Company.

Queen Victoria didn't think the Kohinoor had enough brilliance and ordered it recut. The foremost cutter of his time, a Hollander named Voorsanger, was called to London for the job and installed in the workshop of the royal jewelers. After thirty-eight days of labor, the Kohinoor was reduced from 186 to 108.93 carats. It was considered a poor job; the diamond no longer looked like the stone which had so much history, and the new cutting failed to give it the expected brilliancy.

Queen Victoria wore it as a brooch, but after her death it was transferred to the crown of Queen Mary. Then it was set in the crown made in 1937 for the coronation of Elizabeth, who became the Queen Mother.

The great stone is on display with the other Crown Jewels in the Tower of London. It is a moving experience to see the stone—not for its looks, as it is not a beauty and is far outsparkled by other gems in the collection, but because of its history. As I viewed the Kohinoor, I recalled the violence, hundreds of years of it, and the romance and lust and passion that make it the incomparable Kohinoor, a diamond whose history is without equal.

THE DARYA-I-NUR

The best known gem in Iran is the Darya-i-Nur or the

The best-known gem in Iran, Darya-i-Nur, the "sea of light," part of the booty from the sack of Delhi in 1739. Credit: Royal Ontario Museum

"sea of light." It was part of the booty, along with the Kohinoor ("mountain of light") and the Peacock Throne, which Nadir Shah carried off after the sack of Delhi in 1739.

The Darya-i-Nur is the largest pink diamond in existence and one of the world's most sizable. It is rectangular and without internal flaws. Its estimated weight is between 175 and 195 carats. The exact weight cannot be ascertained because it has been in a setting of some kind for years. The diamond is one of several famous ones which came originally from the great Golconda fields of India.

Two years after his triumphant return to Persia with his wagonloads of plunder, Nadir Shah was assassinated. The Darya-i-Nur was inherited by a grandson; then it changed hands several more times before Lutf Ali Khan Zand acquired it. In 1791, an Englishman, Harford Jones, wrote that he saw Zand wearing the Darya-i-Nur and another large diamond, the Taj-E-Mah ("crown of the moon"), in armbands. These stones appear from time to time in Iranian history, but their origins before Nadir Shah brought them back from India are unknown.

In 1642, the ubiquitous Frenchman Tavernier saw a great diamond in India which he named the Great Table because of its flat rectangular shape. He tried unsuccessfully to buy it, or, failing that, to acquire it by other such means as he was known to employ. Subsequently the diamond disappeared. For centuries the Great Table was listed as one of the lost great diamonds.

Now, thanks to a team of Canadian gemologists, it has been established that the Darya-i-Nur is the larger part of the Great Table and that it had been broken in at least two pieces. The break must have occurred prior to 1834, when it was learned the stone was recut by Fath Ali to remove the damaged area. On one of the lower pavilion facets an extra plane was made, probably to cover the break, with the inscription, "As Sultan *SAHIB QIRAN FATH ALI SHAH QAJAR* 1250" (A. D. 1834), the year of his death.

Another diamond named Nur ul-ain ("light of the

eye"), the central stone in Empress Farah's crown, matches the Darya-i-Nur in color and interior quality. Its weight of 60 carats was a factor in establishing it as the other piece from the Great Table. Tavernier placed a weight of 250 carats on the diamond in 1642.

The Darya-i-Nur has a recorded history of over 325 years. The Persian Nasser ed-din-Shah contended that the Great Table was one of the diamonds in the crown of Cyrus the Great (558 to 529 B. C.).

Iain Balfour, the noted British historian of famous diamonds, once reasoned that the peculiar shape of the Darya-i-Nur could allow its being cut at one time. The latest evidence proves his conjecture correct.

Solving the mystery of its fate after its identity was lost for centuries has been a delight for diamond buffs. The Darya-i-Nur was proudly worn by the Shah of Iran, Mohammed Reza Shah Dahlari Aryameht, at his coronation in 1967.

THE CULLINAN

The world's largest gem diamond, the Cullinan, was found by Frederick Wells, superintendent of the Premier Mine in South Africa on January 25, 1905. He was making a routine check of the mine at the end of the day when he sighted the reflection of the setting sun glinting off the wall of a shaft. Upon investigation he found what appeared to be a large crystal, partly uncovered.

With a knife, he dug away the ground in which it was embedded. The more he dug, the more of the crystal appeared. The Premier Mine had provided many large diamonds, but nothing like this had ever been seen, so Mr. Wells decided that someone had planted a large piece of glass to fool someone. Tricks at the mine were an old story.

But he kept digging away. Finally he dislodged the stone, which was as big as his fist. He was afraid to report it immediately in case some of the jokesters might be waiting to see him bring his "find" to the manager's office. So

The world's largest gem diamond, Cullinan I, was found in South Africa in 1905. The Cullinan scepter stone is 2⅛ inches long. Credit: Her Majesty's Stationery Office, London

he had it checked privately and learned the stunning news that it was, indeed, a diamond. Quoting from a letter to me from the Premier Mine, "Fred Wells was a very quiet type of fellow, so when he took the stone up to hand to William McHardy, he was kept waiting because the manager was busy."

One hour later—and richer by a $10,000 reward —Frederick Wells left the office with the knowledge that his find would make history. What he didn't know at the time was that the diamond was, unbelievably, flawless and with a fine limpid color. The stone weighed 3106 carats or 1 ⅓ pounds avoirdupois. The crystal had three natural faces, with the fourth a cleavage, indicating that the stone was larger originally.

It was called the Cullinan Diamond after Thomas Cullinan, the founder and first chairman of the Premier Diamond Mining Co., Ltd.

The gem was to be sent to London. Two armed policemen were to escort the boxed stone from Johannesburg to Cape Town by train and on board a Union Castle ship to Southampton, then by train to London, where it would be delivered to the Bank of England. Photographs showing the policemen going aboard the liner with their box were published in many newspapers. However, unknown even to the policemen, the diamond was sent in another box by registered mail to London.

At Prime Minister Botha's suggestion, the diamond was bought by the Transvaal government and presented to King Edward VII of England on his sixty-sixth birthday as a token of the colony's appreciation for its newly granted constitution. The stone was presented to Edward in its original state. The monarch decided to entrust its cutting to the famed house of Asscher Brothers in Amsterdam. Previously the same firm had cut the Excelsior, the largest diamond ever found prior to the Cullinan. The two Asscher brothers had a private conference with the king in London to discuss the best possible way of cutting the stone before it was mailed to the firm's offices.

When we visited the Asscher plant a few years ago, I was given a booklet which tells the story of the care that went into the cutting. "Special tools," the booklet states,

> had to be made for the cleaving and polishing, as no standard equipment was available for so large a stone. A party of police was permanently present during the whole year that the diamond was in the factory.
>
> On February 10, 1908, in the presence of representatives of the King of Britain, some authorized experts, and a notary public, who was to make an official report of the event, the destiny of the Cullinan was to be decided by the blow of the cleaving-hammer. This cleaving had been prepared for weeks; the possibilities of the stone had been minutely in-

vestigated, and Mr. J. Asscher had needed a fortnight merely for making the incision on the giant stone. Never in the history of diamond working did so much depend on one cleaving. It can, therefore, be understood that the cleaving of the Cullinan, upon which the eyes of the world were fixed, was anticipated by all those concerned, and not least by Mr. J. Asscher, who was to carry out the manipulation.

The booklet does not mention what I consider a very human touch—that a doctor and two nurses were in attendance. If Asscher's calculations were incorrect, the priceless diamond could shatter into a million pieces. Or it might split along lines other than planned. The tension in the room must have been unbearable.

Asscher inserted a steel blade into the groove, took a deep breath, and without further hesitation lifted his rod and struck the blade a sharp blow. The blade shattered, but the diamond remained intact. Without betraying the emotions which must have seethed within him, Asscher calmly inserted a new blade and struck again. This time the stone split exactly as he wished. *It was the most productive blow of all time.*

He spent several ensuing weeks in a hospital recovering from the nervous strain he had been under.

When Louis Asscher, nephew of the man who cleaved the stone, and I were discussing the Cullinan, he said, "I don't understand why all the historians and writers stress the doctor and nurses. My uncle knew exactly what would occur, and there was no question at any time."

That may be very true, but then why were the doctor and nurses on hand? One writer, Robert M. Shipley, the founder of the Gemological Institute of America, in his *Famous Diamonds of the World,* says a San Franciscan who was employed in the factory at the time "reports that after the second blow, a tremendous success, Mr. Asscher fainted." None can blame him.

Further cleaving, sawing, and polishing produced nine major stones, ninety-six minor ones, and 10 carats of polished fragments. The largest, a pear-shape gem 2 ⅛" long, 1 ¾" wide, and 1" thick at its greatest dimension, is the largest cut diamond in existence. Called Cullinan I, it weighs 530.20 carats and is indescribably beautiful. It is set in the royal scepter on display with the other British Crown Jewels.

The Cullinan II, weighing 317.4 carats, the second largest cut diamond in the world, is a cushion-shaped stone set in the band of the Imperial State Crown, also in the Tower of London. Cullinan III, 94.5 carats, is a pear shape set in the finial of Queen Mary's crown. In the band of the same crown rests Cullinan IV, a square cut stone of 63 carats.

In all, nine diamonds cut from the mammoth stone are either in the Crown Jewels or in the personal possession of the British Royal Family.

My wife and I received a signal honor some time ago when we were given a private showing of the Crown Jewels. Looking at them as closely as it is possible to do so, they are every bit as beautiful and as fine in color as they are reputed to be. The occasion was, to a lover of diamonds, a tremendous experience.

THE REGENT

This historic diamond was found by a slave in 1701 in a mine on the Kistna River near Golconda, India. It weighed 410 carats, one of the last large diamonds to come from that famous diamond field. At the risk of his life, the slave slashed the calf of his leg and secreted the stone under the bandages. Fleeing to the seacoast, he made a deal with a ship captain for passage to another Indian port in return for half what the diamond would bring. Once at sea, the slave predictably "fell" overboard and was drowned. The captain sold the diamond to an Indian gem dealer for $5000. Legend has it that the captain spent the proceeds in riotous living, then in a fit of remorse killed himself—although this last seems a bit improbable.

An Indian merchant named Ramchund, in 1702, offered the stone to Thomas Pitt, governor of Madras, for

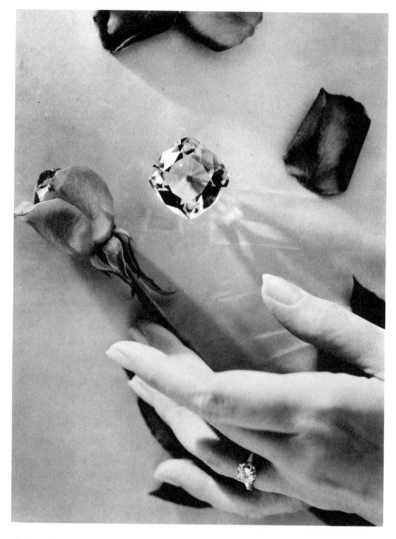

A slave found the historic Regent diamond in India in 1701. It weighed 410 carats. Credit: N. W. Ayer & Son, Inc.

$500,000. Pitt, the grandfather of William Pitt, after whom Pittsburgh, Pennsylvania, was named, was allowed to keep the stone for several weeks while they haggled over the price. Pitt sensed that the stone was a stolen one, so he drove a hard bargain. He finally got it for $100,000. It was no small sum for a diamond in those days.

The stone was sent to England, where it was cut into a beautiful cushion-shaped gem weighing 140.5 carats, and at the time it was named the Pitt. Such a remarkable job of cutting was done that its beauty and brilliance could not have been greater had it been cut by today's skilled artisans. This is all the more remarkable because eighteenth-century jewelers did not have diamond saws and other modern aids. The fashioning took two years to complete.

In 1717, Pitt sold the diamond to the Duke of Orléans, then Regent of France, during the minority of Louis XV. After this sale, the stone became known as the Regent, its present name. Pitt received substantially more than $500,000 for it, thus establishing the family fortune.

The stone was placed in the crown of Louis XV, and it became known as the most valuable in Europe. In the time of Louis XVI, when the crown jewels were worn as personal adornments, his wife, Marie Antoinette, displayed the Regent on a velvet hat. In an inventory of the French treasury, the Regent was valued at $2,500,000 at that time.

It was stolen in the famous French jewel robbery of 1792 along with other famous gems. Unlike the famous Blue Diamond, which was part of the loot, the Regent was recovered almost immediately. In 1796, it was used as collateral to German bankers to buy cavalry equipment. Redeemed in 1797, it was pawned again the next year to foreign bankers to help finance Napoleon's bid for power. Five years later, Bonaparte redeemed the stone and had it mounted in the hilt of his ceremonial sword for his coronation as emperor in Notre Dame Cathedral.

After Napoleon was exiled, the Regent continued to be involved in political affairs. It was carried by his second wife, Empress Marie Louise, to the château of Blois in her home in Austria. Her father, Emperor Francis II of Austria, returned the diamond to the French government.

Louis XVIII fled with it to Ghent in 1815, but brought it back when he ascended the French throne after Waterloo. After his death, his brother, Charles X, wore the Regent

The Regent mounted in Napoleon's sword. Credit: B. T. Batsford, Ltd.

for his coronation in 1825. Then Napoleon III had a diadem designed for Empress Eugénie with the Regent set in it. In 1887, when France needed money again, the crown jewels were auctioned. But because of its historic value, the Regent was paid the tribute of being excluded from the sale and was placed in the Louvre as a national treasure. When the Germans invaded Paris in 1940, the Regent was hidden in the château country near Chambord. After the war, it was returned to its place of honor in the Louvre.

THE ORLOFF

The greatest jewel in the fabulously valuable Diamond Treasury of the Soviet Union is the gem known

The greatest gem in the diamond treasury of the Soviet Union is the Orloff.
Credit: N. W. Ayer & Son, Inc.

as the Orloff. It first came to the attention of Westerners
about 1750, when it was learned that in the southern Indian state of Mysore there was a Brahmin temple which
contained an idol with two huge diamonds for eyes. A
French grenadier, a deserter of the Carnatic wars in India,
lived in the neighborhood of the temple and was the first
to hear about the great treasure. No Christian was allowed

in the temple, so the Frenchman went native and professed to embrace the Brahmin faith. He first obtained employment within the walls. After several years, he was permitted to worship at the inner shrine. Eventually he became one of the trusted guardians of the idol.

One stormy night when no worshiper was present, he pried out one of the diamond eyes. But while he was working on the other he heard a noise, lost his nerve, and fled with the one huge diamond. He made his way to

Catherine the Great gladly accepted the Orloff diamond from a former lover—but she never wore it. Credit: N. W. Ayer & Son, Inc.

Madras on the Bay of Bengal, where he found English troops and safety.

He had no trouble disposing of the diamond. A British sea captain offered him $10,000 for it, no questions asked. The skipper in 1775, sold the stone in London for $60,000 to a Persian merchant named Khojeh. It is not known whether the Persian or someone else finally sold it to Prince Gregory Orloff for a reputed $450,000.

Orloff had been one of the Russian officers who engineered the coup through which Catherine the Great seized the throne in 1762. He was her favorite during the early days of her rule, but with the passing years she

The Orloff diamond was mounted in Catherine's royal scepter. The stone weighs almost 200 carats. Credit: B. T. Batsford, Ltd.

turned to other lovers. The Russian court was gay and exciting at this time, but Orloff was not part of it, as he had displeased Catherine with his bungling of a political matter and had lost his high position.

Seeking to regain Catherine's favor, Orloff and his brothers, all of whom were reputed former lovers of the queen, pooled their resources and bought the great diamond. At the feast of her name day in 1776, he presented the diamond to her instead of the traditional bouquet. She accepted it happily enough. A great admirer of diamonds, she was said to have over 2500 of them in her crown, many of them cut in her own laboratory in the Ural Mountains. But she never wore the diamond Prince Orloff gave her, nor did she ever reinstate his family to their former high positions, so it was a great gamble which lost.

Catherine had the diamond mounted in her royal scepter. The diamond was called the Orloff in honor of its donor. The stone is shaped like half a small hard-boiled egg, rose cut at the top and flat at the bottom. It is ⅞" high, 1¼" wide, and 1⅜" long. Its weight is now 199.60 carats.

Some experts believe the Orloff is the same stone once known as the Great Mogul Diamond. Tavernier was the only European who reported having seen the latter stone, which disappeared after Nadir Shah's sack of Delhi in 1739. The Great Mogul was far heavier than the Orloff, but it could have been cut down into several smaller stones, or it may have been lost forever. It is unlikely that anyone will ever know.

THE JONKER

Jacobus Jonker (pronounced "Yonker"), a veteran but luckless diamond digger for most of his sixty-two years, was walking on his humble farm near Pretoria, South Africa, after a heavy storm to see if the rain had washed up anything. This was an old habit of his, but it had never produced a thing. On this occasion, January 17, 1934, he spied on the ground a mud-covered stone the size of a hen's egg.

The Jonker diamond, found in the mud in South Africa by Jacobus Jonker in 1934. He sold the stone for $315,000. Credit: N. W. Ayer & Son, Inc.

From habit, Jonker picked it up and wiped it off. It had every appearance of a diamond in the rough. Trembling with excitement, he dashed home to show it to his wife and seven children. Of course, he couldn't be sure. He had never seen a diamond anywhere near that large, and the "skin" around it made identification difficult. His wife tied it in a cloth and took it to bed with her, but she didn't sleep a wink that night. Jonker and his oldest son stood guard at the door, although no one outside the family knew anything about the stone.

A few days later he sold the gem for $315,000 to a dealer for the Diamond Corporation in Johannesburg. The great stone, the seventh largest ever found, weighed 726 carats, just .60 of a carat less than the Presidente Vargas, the sixth largest, found in Brazil in 1938. The Jonker proved to be a magnificent gem of finest quality and color. The diamond was sent to London by ordinary mail at a cost of sixty-four cents. Harry Winston, who figures so prominently in the handling of great stones, heard about it, cabled to London for an option, and reached the city at the same time as the diamond. He studied the stone for a month and purchased it for an undisclosed sum, although one authority puts the figure at $700,000. Buying a rough of this size is a great gamble which can pay handsome dividends or end in a huge loss.

From the Custom House in New York, the package containing the Jonker, as it was now called, was sent directly to the Museum of Natural History. The diamond was immediately put on exhibition. Visitors stood in long lines to get a view. Later, it was shown in six other cities, each time to large crowds.

After getting the opinions of the great European cutters as to how they would cleave the stone, Winston returned the Jonker to the United States and sought the advice of Lazare Kaplan, a Belgian who had moved to New York. Following long study, Kaplan said he would cleave it in a manner different from the way the Europeans had suggested. Winston asked Kaplan to do the job his way.

Kaplan hesitated. He was already a legend as a master cutter and he had a very successful business. It would take months to study the stone, he would have to make hundreds of models, and, if his calculations proved wrong, his reputation, as well as that of American cutters generally, would suffer. Still, no great stone like the Jonker had ever been cut in the United States. It represented a challenge which Kaplan could not turn down. He made models of the Jonker and studied them for a year. Just when he thought he had pinpointed the exact spot for cleavage, he observed a microscopic bend in a surface crack. This made it necessary to alter his calculations and to study the crystallization further.

Finally, after more months of study, more models, and diagrams, he told Winston that he was ready. Kaplan stated that the stone would yield eleven emerald-cut stones including one very large one, plus a marquise-shaped stone. He took off a few days to rest.

Then, with his son, Leo, by his side to assist, Kaplan dealt the all-important blow. The diamond fell apart exactly as he anticipated.

Lazare Kaplan, who cleaved the Jonker diamond, at his bench. Credit: Lazare Kaplan & Sons

Lazare Kaplan's grandson, Peter, in a letter to me provided some interesting sidelights which I quote:

> The Europeans thought the cleavage plane was parallel to the large flat surface that the stone would naturally sit on. However, my grandfather, through careful study of the crystallography of the diamond, saw that this was not the case. If the stone had been cleaved the way the European experts had recommended, the stone would probably have shattered into many fragments.
>
> The "rest" that my grandfather took was a trip to his farm in upstate New York, where he spent the weekend in one of his favorite hobbies, namely, trout fishing.
>
> My grandfather gave a mighty blow to the cleaving knife, not a mere tap. I am sure that you realize that the larger the stone the greater the blow to the cleaving knife. The greatness of the cleave was such that there was ink on both sides of the cleave and two large pieces with mirror-like planes resulted.

The largest stone, called the Jonker Diamond, weighs 125.65 carats and is the largest emerald-cut diamond in the world. It was exhibited in many parts of the country and drew crowds greater than when it was in its rough state.

The Jonker was sold by Winston to King Farouk of Egypt, but later repossessed. It then became the property of the Queen of Nepal, but sometime after 1959, when it was last corroborated, all traces of it were lost. Finally, it was learned that in 1972 a Hong Kong jeweler sold it to a Japanese businessman whose identity is not known. The reputed price paid for the Jonker was $3,500,000, undoubtedly the highest ever paid for a single cut and fashioned diamond.

Three of the other stones cut from the rough of this stone were sold to a Maharajah of Indore and the others to private owners.

THE IDOL'S EYE

The Idol's Eye is a beautiful white, semi-round diamond which was found late in the sixteenth or at the beginning of the seventeenth century, most likely in the

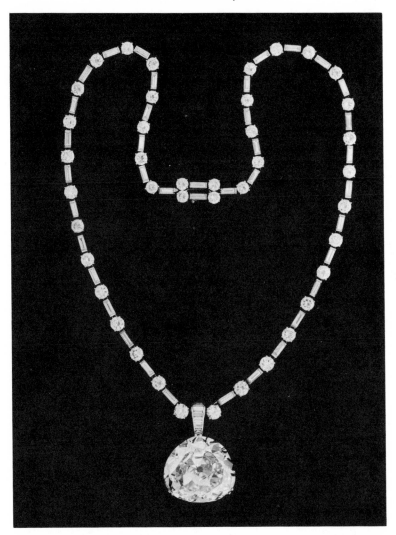

The Idol's Eye, a beautiful white diamond, was found in the famous Golconda fields in India. Credit: N. W. Ayer & Son, Inc.

famous Golconda fields in India. Possessed of a rare bluish tinge and weighing 70.20 carats in its present form, it was once the eye of a sacred idol in a beautiful temple. There are conflicting reports about the temple's location, but most authorities agree it was in a place called Benghazi in northern Libya. People are reported to have come from

Abdul Hamid II, Sultan of Turkey, came into possession of the Idol's Eye in the early 1900s. Credit: Brown Bros.

afar to worship in the temple and to gaze with awe at what they considered a sacred stone.

The Idol's Eye became the property of the Persian prince Rahab very early in its history. He was in debt to the East India Company, which seized the diamond in 1607 for non-payment. Nearly two and a half centuries later, in 1849, the East India Company seized another huge diamond, the Kohinoor, as partial indemnity of the Sikh wars.

In any case, after its acquisition by the East India Company, the Idol's Eye disappeared from public view. Nothing was known of it for exactly 300 years. Then, in 1907, it was found to be in the possession of the Turkish

Sultan Abdul Hamid II. How it got into his treasury is a mystery, but there are a number of fanciful stories.

One of the Sultan's predecessors, according to a widespread if unsupported version, abducted the beautiful Princess Rasheetah right under the nose of her lover, the Sheik of Kashmir. The Idol's Eye, the Sheik's most treasured gem, was used as ransom for the safe return of the Princess, and some time later it became part of Hamid's trove. This story fails to explain how the Sheik got the stone from the East India Company, a formidable task in itself.

It was about 1907 that Sultan Abdul Hamid II was having troubles at home at the hands of the "Young Turks." Fearing that a coup d'état was imminent, he conspired with his Grand Vizier to smuggle his important jewels, which included the Idol's Eye and the Hope Diamond, out of the country and into France.

The Grand Vizier, in the tradition of such stories, secretly planned to get the jewels for himself and enlisted the aid of a trusted young man. Following the Grand Vizier's instructions, he boarded the train to Paris and carefully hid the jewels. Waiting for the train to stop at a certain station, he shot himself and inflicted a slight wound. Then he raised a terrible hue and cry, shouting that he had been robbed of his jewels and the thieves had fled into the station. During the excitement, he retrieved the jewels and hid them on his person. So far, so good. But now he double crossed the Grand Vizier. Once in Paris, he took the gems to a fence and ran off with the proceeds. The Turkish Secret Police never did capture him.

Such fanciful tales so often attach themselves to famous gems, but there is no doubt that the Idol's Eye did reach Paris in 1907 and was sold to a Spanish nobleman.

The Idol's Eye changed hands several times and during World War II was sent to the United States for safekeeping. It was eventually acquired by Harry Winston, who sold it to Mrs. May Bonfils Stanton of Denver. She considered it her most special and favorite diamond. When her estate jewelry was auctioned at the Parke-

Bernet galleries in New York in 1962, the famous diamond was obtained by Harry Levinson, a Chicago jeweler. It is valued at $1,000,000.

THE KASICKI

The pride of the Topkapi Palace Museum in Istanbul, Turkey, and its most valuable single exhibit, is the 86-carat pear-shaped "Spoon Maker" Diamond, also known as the Kasicki. Surrounded by a double row of round-cut diamonds and well spotlighted, it hangs in a glass case on the wall of one of the rooms of the Treasury.

Its origin is not clear. Like many other historic diamonds, it is difficult to separate fact from fancy. Rasid,

The pride of the Topkapi Palace Museum in Istanbul, and its most valuable single exhibit, is the 86-carat Spoon Maker diamond, also known as Kasicki. Credit: Topkapi Museum

the official historian of the Ottoman court, describes it thus:

> In the year 1669, a very poor man found a pretty stone in the rubbish heap of Egrikapi in Istanbul. He bartered it to a spoon-maker for three wooden spoons. The spoon-maker sold this stone to a jeweler for ten silver coins.
>
> The jeweler consulted another jeweler who knew immediately that the pretty stone was really a precious diamond. When the second jeweler threatened to disclose the whole matter, the two men quarreled bitterly. Another jeweler heard the story and bought the diamond, giving a purse full of money to each of the angry jewelers. But now the Grand Vizier, Köprülüzade Ahmed Pasha, has heard of the gem. When Sultan Mehmed IV is told of the affair, he orders the stone to be brought to the palace, and he takes possession of it. Whether he paid for it is not revealed. And, of course, no one knows what history preceded its being thrown into the garbage heap.

A more probable story is that in 1774 a French officer named Pikot bought the diamond from the Maharajah of Madras in India and took it to France. Somehow thieves got wind of the gem and robbed Pikot.

Some time later a large diamond, about the size of the stone taken from Pikot, appeared at an auction, and the notorious Casanova made a bid for it. The diamond thus became known for a time as the Casanova lottery diamond. It was finally bought by Napoleon's mother, Letizia Ramolino, who later sold her jewels to help her son escape from Elba in 1815.

An officer of Tepedelenli Ali Pasha bought the great diamond for 150,000 pieces of gold and put it in Tepedelenli's Treasury. When he was killed in the revolt against Sultan Mahmut II, his entire treasury came to the Palace of Turkey. It is probable that this stone, now called the Kasicki, is the lost Pikot diamond.

4
Jewels of History

The star of sunset smiles again—a diamond set in gold!
—John Greenleaf Whittier

The fascination of historic royal jewels is due not only to their beauty and value, but also to their association with a nation's gloried past.

Traditions and legends are woven about the tangible jewels proudly displayed by each nation. They have had

The Crown Jewels and Regalia photographed at the Tower of London; *St. Edward's Crown and the Orb*, background, *the scepter with Dove*, left, *the scepter with Cross*, right, and *the Sovereign's Ring*, foreground. *The scepter contains the Great Star of Africa, which was cut from the Cullinan diamond. Crown Copyright Reserved; credit: British Information Services*

60

no small part in the formation of the identity of the country. They represent living proof of power and glory possibly long gone. Few are the objects displayed which equal the glamor and excitement exuded by crown jewels.

This is particularly true in countries where the royal family still commands love and respect, such as England and Iran. No one who has seen the long patient line of Britons waiting for hours outside the Tower of London for a chance to glimpse the Crown Jewels will ever under-estimate the magic of diamonds and their relationship to the history and glory of their nation.

Since Biblical times, crowns have been worn as sym-

Queen Elizabeth II holds the royal scepter and orb, part of the magnificent British Crown Jewels. Credit: Wide World Photos

bols of authority or nobility. In ancient Egypt and Assyria they represented authority or nobility. The early Greeks used them to crown victors of athletic events. Mostly the old crowns were made of wreaths, but when, later, the Romans adopted the custom, the emperor Aurelian wore pearls on a ribbon tied to his head. It was but a short step to Constantine's use of precious metal, probably gold, to form a headband. Then precious gems were added.

As dynasties prospered, their collections of gems reached such proportions that they could no longer be confined to crowns. So swords and scabbards became jewel encrusted, which in turn led to other jewel-bearing items for military or other use. These collections eventually became national treasures.

Some gems were purchased and presented to sovereigns as gestures of love and loyalty, notably the Cullinan diamonds of England. At the other extreme, the great Kohinoor has a history of intrigue and bloodshed unequaled by any other diamond. Ironically, both are on display close to each other in the Tower of London.

In times of glory, crown jewels were worn by royalty on state occasions. In times of stress, the gems of the empire saved the nation from financial collapse. The French crown jewels, for example, were valued at 30,000,000 francs when Louis XVI sold them in desperation in 1792 to support the nation's shaky paper currency. Even today the fabulous collection of jewels in Iran's treasury is used to back its currency.

The British crown jewels are probably the world's greatest and most valuable collection of diamonds. Yet how can anyone place a value on gems of such great historic and sentimental value? Diamonds like the Cullinan and the Kohinoor tell in eloquent silence stories of the great and historic events of the nation as nothing else can.

By contrast to the magnificent British crown jewels, those of Scotland, displayed in the Crown Room in Edinburgh Castle, would be something of a letdown if one were looking only for visual glamour. The three main pieces are the royal crown, scepter, and state sword and

Queen Mary's crown is set with the famous Kohinoor and Cullinan's III and IV. Credit: British Information Services

are known as the Honors. They can be traced to King Alexander III (1249–1286), although parts of the actual pieces are from an earlier period. Scotland's last coronation was that of Charles II in 1651.

Even though Scotland is now part of Great Britain, the Scots have stubbornly retained their identity and their jewels as a reminder of the time they enjoyed their own sovereignty.

In 1817, Sir Walter Scott received a warrant from King George IV of Britain to display the royal Scottish regalia in the Crown Room of the castle, where they have remained ever since. What a story they could tell! They are a perfect example of the contention that the value of crown jewels cannot be measured in dollars alone, for the pride and

DIAMONDS ETERNAL

history of Scotland is reflected by them in a way which reaches the hearts of all who view them.

The Crown Jewels of Scotland on display in Edinburgh. Credit: B. T. Batsford, Ltd.

The Imperial Crown of Russia was originally ordered for the coronation of Catherine the Great in 1762. It contains 4936 diamonds weighing 2858 carats. Credit: B. T. Batsford, Ltd.

Soviet Russia was quick to rid the country of customs and traditions associated with the czars, but the imperial family's vast collection of jewels has remained largely intact in the Kremlin. The diamonds in this treasure are

A diamond necklace, one of thousands of pieces in the Russian treasury, has thirty-six large diamonds, weighing a total of more than 475 carats, an average of 13 carats each. Credit: B. T. Batsford, Ltd.

measured in thousands of carats, and the collection is classified as one of the world's most important. The Soviets, too, know the sentimental value of the royal jewels.

Until 1960, the crown jewels of Iran, a treasure of gigantic proportions, were kept hidden, and only on rare occasions did an outsider get to view them. In December

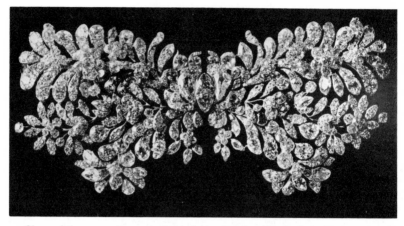

Clasp of the coronation mantle made for Tsarina Elizabeth in 1750. The total weight of diamonds is almost 400 carats. Credit: B. T. Batsford, Ltd.

of that year, His Imperial Majesty Muhammad Reza Shah opened a display of the choicest pieces. Although the gallery is protected by thick walls, great steel doors, electronic alarm, automatic gates, and armed guards, it does not give the impression of being a vault. This is described fully by authors Meen and Tushingham in their book *Crown Jewels of Iran*. The exhibit includes a number of tiaras and thousands of cut but unset diamonds, many of important size.

The Pahlavi Crown is one of the main attractions. His Imperial Majesty Muhammad Reza Shah Pahlavi Aryamihr donned this crown at his coronation in 1967. It is set with 3380 diamonds, the largest weighing about 60 carats, as well as pearls and other gems.

The bulk of the important gems in the collection represents what survives of Nadir Shah's booty taken from Delhi in 1739, when Iran was known as Persia. The crown jewels of Iran are not the personal property of the reigning family, but belong to the state and are used to back up the currency. For affairs of state, certain jewels are made available, but they must be returned like Cinderella's finery after the ball.

Another immensely valuable collection is that of the

The Pahlavi Crown was worn by the Shah of Iran on his coronation in 1967. Credit: The National Bank of Teheran, Iran

Ottoman Empire on display in the famed Topkapi Sarayi Museum in Istanbul. These gems were gathered during the period when Ottoman sultans extended their influence across vast stretches of Europe, Asia, and Africa, and lesser potentates paid tribute with gifts of precious stones.

The museum handbook explains: "This valuable Treasury was formed from the following: War booty, the gifts of foreign ambassadors, the offerings of countries under the protection of the Empire, the presents sent for weddings and circumcision feasts, the valuables taken over by the government after the death of important people in the government, and the items which were bought."

Vases, bowls, headdresses, swords, and many other pieces in the exhibit, all heavily studded with diamonds and precious stones, obviously were seized as booty. Their age is shown by the old form of cutting. I don't recall seeing any diamonds of modern cut. One famous piece is

A vase, with diamonds, from the Topkapi Sarayi Museum in Istanbul. Credit: Topkapi Museum

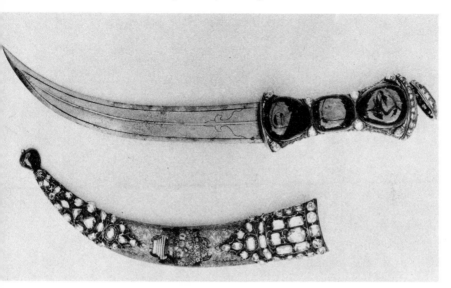

The famous emerald-and-diamond dagger that was used in the motion picture Topkapi *several years ago. Credit: Topkapi Museum*

the emerald and diamond dagger used in the motion picture *Topkapi*, filmed several years ago. The dagger has a hinged top which, when open, displays a watch.

Turkey's greatest diamond, the 86-carat, pear-shaped "Spoon Maker" is prominently displayed on a wall. Another unusual piece is a canopied throne only seven inches high, on which is seated a sultan whose body is formed by what is claimed to be the world's largest pearl.

Over the years, I have found that some of the most treasured gems are not particularly large. They depend on their history for their value. As a matter of fact, many of the largest diamonds are relatively unknown. Very large diamonds are a rarity; fewer than 100 are known to have weighed 200 carats or more at the time they were found.

Undoubtedly there were many more, particularly those of Indian origin, as the records of the original weights are lacking in many cases. For instance, there is no record of the rough from which such famous stones as the Hope, the Kohinoor, and the Orloff were cut. Some of the early Brazilian stones probably suffered the same fate.

Many of the largest rough diamonds were never named. They were simply cut and marketed.

More than half of those on the list of largest stones were found in this century, which indicates the record is far from complete—and never will be. Today, however, we can be sure that when a large one is found, no matter in which country, it will be duly noted.

Most of the large diamonds discovered brought rewards to the finders—money today, but formerly land and cattle, and, in really olden times, freedom from forced labor in the fields.

On February 14, 1972, what is reported to be the third largest known rough diamond was found on a conveyer belt in the mines of Sierra Leone. It weighed 968.90 carats and was named the Star of Sierra Leone. After being displayed in the National Museum in Freeport, the capital of Sierra Leone, it was sold to Harry Winston, who was in no hurry to have it cut.

The Star of Sierra Leone, the third largest diamond ever found, was discovered in West Africa on February 14, 1972. It weighs 968.9 carats and measures 2 ½ inches × 1 ½ inches. Credit: N. W. Ayer & Son, Inc.

The largest diamond by far is the Cullinan, with an unbelievable weight, when found, of 3106 carats—1 1/3 pounds avoirdupois. Only two others came close to 1000 carats—the Excelsior, which weighed 995.20 carats, and the Star of Sierra Leone.

The loss in cutting and fashioning diamonds is considerable. Here's what happened to the two largest:

The Excelsior produced twenty-one finished gems. The largest, named the Excelsior, weighed 69.80 carats. Three weighed over 40 carats, six weighed from 13.86 to 34.91, with the rest descending to less than a carat. The combined weight of the cut stones was 373.75 carats, or three-eighths of the weight of the rough. The balance, 62½ percent, was reduced to fragments or dust.

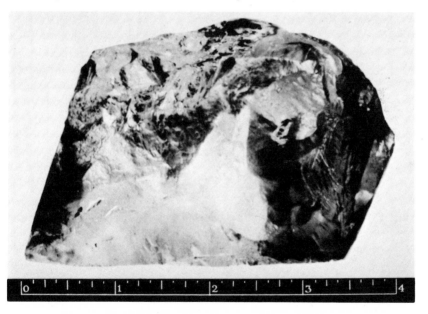

The Cullinan rough. Credit: Asscher Diamond Cutting Works, Amsterdam

The Cullinan, in cut form, produced the largest cut diamond in the world, 530.20 carats. This makes it larger than all but sixteen of the largest in rough form. The same crystal also produced the second largest cut diamond in existence, 317.40 carats. This, too, takes a respectable place when compared to the rough stones listed. The total weight of the cut gems came to 1063 carats, and the loss, after cutting, was more than sixty-five percent.

But the incomparable thrill of discovering one of these immense diamonds must have been present in every case.

Following are lists of the fifty largest uncut diamonds and the fifty-three cut diamonds weighing 100 carats or more. Of the fifty-three, twenty-eight have been lost or their present owners are not known for certain.

FIFTY LARGEST KNOWN ROUGH GEM DIAMONDS

Weight (carats)	Name	Color	When Found	Where Found
3106.00	Cullinan	White	1905	South Africa
995.20	Excelsior	White	1893	South Africa
968.90	Star of Sierra Leone	White	1972	Sierra Leone
787.50	Great Mogul	White	1650	India
770.00	Woyie River	White	1945	Sierra Leone
726.60	Presidente Vargas	White	1938	Brazil
726.00	Jonker	White	1934	South Africa
650.80	Reitz	White	1895	South Africa
620.14	Anon.	White	1970	South Africa
609.25	Baumgold Rough	White	1922	South Africa
601.25	Lesotho	Brown	1967	Lesotho
600.00	Goyaz	White	1906	Brazil
600.00	Anon.	White	1884	South Africa
593.50	Anon.	White	1919	South Africa
572.25	Anon.	White	1955	South Africa
567.75	Anon.	White	1912	South Africa
537.00	Anon.	White	Unknown	South Africa
532.00	Anon.	White	1943	Sierra Leone
527.00	Lesotho B	White	1965	Lesotho
523.74	Anon.	White	1907	South Africa
514.00	Anon.	White	1911	South Africa

FIFTY LARGEST KNOWN ROUGH GEM DIAMONDS (cont.)

Weight (carats)	Name	Color	When Found	Where Found
511.25	Venter	Yellow	1951	South Africa
507.00	Anon.	White	1914	South Africa
503.50	Anon.	White	1896	South Africa
490.00	Baumgold II	Yellow	1941	South Africa
487.25	Anon.	White	1905	South Africa
469.00	Victoria 1884	White	1884	South Africa
458.75	Anon.	White	1907	South Africa
458.00	Anon.	White	1913	South Africa
455.00	Darcy Vargas	Brown	1939	Brazil
444.00	Anon.	White	1926	South Africa
442.25	Anon.	White	1917	South Africa
440.00	Nizam	White	1835	India
435.00	Light of Peace	White	1969	Sierra Leone*
430.50	Anon.	White	1913	South Africa
428.50	Victoria 1880	Yellowish	1880	South Africa
428.50	DeBeers	Yellowish	1888	South Africa
427.50	Anon.	White	1913	South Africa
426.50	Ice Queen	White	1954	South Africa
419.00	Anon.	White	1913	South Africa
416.25	Berglen	Brown	1924	South Africa
412.50	Broderick	Unknown	1928	South Africa
410.00	Pitt (Regent)	White	1701	India
407.68	Presidente Dutra	White	1949	Brazil
407.50	Anon.	White	1926	South Africa
400.65	Coromandel	Unknown	1948	Brazil
400.00	DeBeers	White	1891	South Africa
381.00	Arc	Unknown	1921	South Africa
375.10	Diario Minas Gerais	Unknown	1941	Brazil
375.00	Red Cross	Yellow	1917	South Africa

* Estimated

LARGEST CUT DIAMONDS, Schedule I

Weight (carats)	Name	Color	Shape	Present Location and Owner	Date Corrob- orated
530.20	Cullinan I	White	Pear	British Crown Jewels, London	1971
317.40	Cullinan II	White	Cushion	British Crown Jewels, London	1971
277.00	Nizam	White	Dome	Nizam of Hyderabad, India	1934
245.35	Jubilee	White	Cushion	Paul-Louis Weiller, Paris	1971
199.60	Orloff	White	Rose Cut	Russian Diamond Treasury, Moscow	1968
185.00*	Darya-i-Nur	Pink	Table Cut	Iranian Treasury, Teheran	1968
152.16	Iranian A	Yellow	Cushion	Iranian Treasury, Teheran	1968
148.00	Nawanager	White	Round	Rajmata Gulabkunverba, Nawanager	1970
140.50	Regent	White	Cushion	The Louvre, Paris	1971
135.45	Iranian B	Yellow	Cushion	Iranian Treasury, Teheran	1968
130.27	Light of Peace	White	Pear	Zale Corporation, Dallas	1971
128.80	Star of the South	White	Oval	Rustomjee Jamsetjee, Bombay	1940
128.51	Tiffany	Golden	Cushion	Tiffany Company, N.Y.	1971
128.25	Niarchos	White	Pear	Stavros P. Niarchos	1966

* Estimated

LARGEST CUT DIAMONDS, Schedule I (cont.)

Weight (carats)	Name	Color	Shape	Present Location and Owner	Date Corroborated
127.02	Portuguese	White	Emerald Cut	Smithsonian Institution, Washington	1971
125.65	Jonker	White	Emerald Cut	Sold to Japanese businessman	1972
123.93	Iranian C	Cape	Cushion	Iranian Treasury, Teheran	1968
121.90	Iranian D	Cape	Multi-faceted partly cut octa-hedron	Iranian Treasury, Teheran	1968
118.05	Meister	Yellow	Cushion	Walter Meister, Zurich	1970
115.06	Taj-e-Mah	White	Rose Cut	Iranian Treasury, Teheran	1968
114.28	Iranian E	Yellow	Cushion	Iranian Treasury, Teheran	1968
111.59	Earth Star	Coffee	Pear	Baumgold Bros., N.Y.	1971
108.93	Kohinoor	White	Oval	British Crown Jewels, London	1971
107.46	Rojtman	Yellow	Cushion	Mrs. Marc Rojtman, N.Y.	1966
104.15	Great Chrysan-themum	Brown	Pear	Julius Cohen, N.Y.	1971

LARGEST CUT DIAMONDS, Schedule II

(100 carats or more, authenticated, but unknown location or owner.)

Weight (carats)	Name	Color	Shape	Last Heard	
280.00	Great Mogul	White	Rose	Lost after sack of Delhi	1739
250.00	Indien	White	Pear	Listed by Duke of Brunswick	1869
234.50	DeBeers	Yellow	Unknown	Sold to unknown Indian Prince	1890
228.50	Victoria 1880	Yellow	Brilliant	Sold to unknown Indian Prince	1882
205.00	Red Cross	Canary Yellow	Square	Sold in London	1918
202.00	Black Star of Africa	Black	Unknown	Exhibited in Tokyo	1971
184.50	Victoria 1884	White	Oval	Nizam of Hyderabad?	1885
183.00	Moon	Yellow	Brilliant	Sold at Sotheby's	1942
150.00	Darya-i-Nur Dacca	White?	Square?	Offered for sale in Dacca	1959
147.00	Turkey I	White?	Square?	Reported in Turkish Crown Jewels	1882
137.27	Florentine	Yellow	Double Rose	Stolen from Austrian Royal Family	1920
136.32	Queen of Holland	White bluish tint	Cushion	Unknown Indian Prince	1925
135.00	Mountain of Splendor	White	Unknown	Persian Crown Jewels	1838
130.00	Great Brazilian	Unknown	Unknown	Shown at Sears' Stores	1956
126.00	Moon of Mountains	White	Unknown	Russian Crown Jewels	1850
123.00	Julius Pam	Yellow	Unknown	Unknown; cut in 1889	1889

LARGEST CUT DIAMONDS, Schedule II (cont.)

Weight (carats)	Name	Color	Shape	Last Heard	
123.00	Stewart	Yellow	Oval/Round	Cut after 1882	1882
114.03	Unnamed	Yellow	Cushion	Sold at Christie's, London	1962
109.26	Cross of Asia	Champagne	Table	Shown by Joske's, San Antonio	1947
107.50	Star of Diamonds	Unknown	Unknown	Reported by Streeter	1882
106.75	Star of Egypt	White?	Emerald cut	Shown in London	1850
106.00	Cent Six	Unknown	Unknown	Reported by Streeter Queen's jeweler	1882
104.88	Deepdene	Yellow	Cushion	Sold by Winston	1954
103.00	Raulconda	White	Unknown	Reported by Tavernier	1650
102.00	Ashberg	Amber	Cushion	Sold in Stockholm	1959
101.00	Hastings	Unknown	Brilliant	Unknown since presented to George III	1786
100.00	Jacob	White	Unknown	Bank of India?	1956
100.00	Star of the East	White	Pear	Unknown since abdication of King Farouk	1952

5

The Queen's Necklace

My, how the diamond did twinkle and glitter by the light of our one candle!
—William Makepeace Thackeray,
The Great Hoggarty Diamond

The two preceding chapters have been devoted to gems surrounded by an aura of romance, history, pride, and tradition. Let me now tell you the story of a notorious piece of diamond jewelry. It's a story of evil and intrigue, greed and double-dealing, of fantastically complicated musical comedy plotting—all involving an ornament known simply as the Queen's Necklace.

Marie Antoinette, whose name is linked with the necklace, never wore it and never wanted it, but she was guillotined because of the wide repercussions it wrought. The necklace also has been blamed for igniting the French Revolution, the beheading of her husband, Louis XVI, and the subsequent death of their young son, Louis XVII. It was instrumental in the disgrace of a famous cardinal and the banishment of others who had a part in the scandal it caused.

It all started innocently enough in 1774. The court jewelers, Böhmer and Bessenger, designed and created the necklace with the thought of selling it to the King, as any merchant with such a customer might have done. The firm ended up bankrupt and Böhmer lost his mind in the bargain. Unwittingly, the jewelers unleashed the forces of terror which changed French history.

The jewelers, well aware that Louis XV showered gifts on his mistress, Madame Du Barry, drew a design for a fabulous diamond necklace and showed it to her. Madame was not slow in voicing her approval. The jewelers went to work on it without getting either the King's approval or a definite order for it. They were certain that these were just formalities since they had sold the King many fine pieces.

Unfortunately, Louis XV died of smallpox soon afterward. The necklace had been started and enough diamonds bought to complete it. The jewelers decided to show it to Louis XVI in its incompleted form with a view to finishing it in time for his coronation the following year.

The necklace has been described as being so large that the case, fifteen by twenty inches, was much too small to show it off at its best. Studded with 647 diamonds, which

The Queen's Necklace, which was associated with Marie Antoinette, contained 647 brilliant stones. Credit: N. W. Ayer & Son, Inc.

weighed almost 3000 carats, it was a piece to defy the imagination. The 603 "smallest" diamonds weighed over four carats each!

In the words of Thomas Carlyle, this was "a glorious ornament fit only for the Sultana of the World." He placed a value of almost $500,000 on it in 1835. Today, it would be valued, according to the description of the quality of the diamonds, at well over $6,000,000. However, André Castelot, in his book *Queen of France*, describes the necklace as "rather ugly, like the collar for a circus horse." In any case, it drew gasps of admiration at the time.

Louis XVI was only too well aware that his Queen, Marie Antoinette, had a passion for diamonds, and he was becoming weary of paying for her extravagant purchases. Perhaps the jewelers caught him in a bad mood. He coldly rejected their proposal.

So much money and effort had been put into the necklace that the jewelers decided to complete it regardless. However, no one in France could afford such a piece. The jewelers, who had strained their credit to complete the necklace, found themselves hard pressed.

When Marie's first child was born, the jewelers thought surely the King would want to celebrate the event with a lavish gift. By-passing the King, they showed the necklace to Marie Antoinette herself. Surprisingly, she turned it down. For the asking price of 1,800,000 francs, she said, France could commission a ship of the line needed because of worsening relations with England.

Böhmer traveled throughout Europe trying in vain to interest royal families in the necklace. Finally he was reduced to hawking the necklace to all comers, offering a commission of 200,000 francs to anyone who could sell the piece. Eventually the jewelers went to a lawyer named La Porte, who was a friend of the Countess de la Motte de Valois, reputed to be a friend of the Queen. Late in 1784, La Porte urged the Countess to intercede for the jewelers, telling her of the enormous commission that would be hers.

The Countess de la Motte de Valois was an enormously complex character. Born Jeanne de Saint-Rémy de Valois in 1756, she was the descendant of an illegitimate son of the impoverished royal House of Valois. Her mother was a beautiful and quick-witted woman who later was reduced to prostitution. Her father died in the poorhouse, and her mother deserted the children.

Jeanne was found begging on the highway by the Marquise de Boulainvilliers, who adopted her. When the Marquise found that the youngster did, indeed, have royal blood, she persuaded Louis XVI to recognize her as of the House of Valois, with the title Mademoiselle de Valois and a small pension from the Crown. Jeanne was placed in a convent school but ran away.

In 1780, she married a soldier, Marc Antoine Nicolas de la Motte, just in time for her to bear twins fathered by the Bishop of Bar Sur Aube. The babies died. In time, Jeanne and her husband called themselves Count and Countess de la Motte de Valois.

Jeanne, at twenty-five, was a very attractive woman. She has been described as a blue-eyed beauty with a fine figure, witty, vivacious, beguiling, and altogether delightful. On the debit side, she was an arch-adventuress, skillful at intrigue, a virtuoso at the gaming tables, and a consummate liar. Perhaps it was natural that she felt she needed a larger field of operations.

Leaving her husband at his army post, she went to Paris, where she wasted little time in making friends and becoming part of the social picture. She spent some time at Court, hoping to be noticed by Marie Antoinette, who made it a point to avoid the newcomer. But, by spreading stories that she was an influential friend of the Queen, Jeanne persuaded people to pay her to intercede for them. Of course, she did nothing for the fees she pocketed. It was at this time that she was contacted by Lawyer La Porte, and together they visited the jewelers to view the necklace.

Her first move was to contact an acquaintance of her husband, Prince Louis-René-Éduard de Rohan, Bishop of Strasbourg, Cardinal of the Holy Church, and member of the Académie Française. Twenty years her senior, the Cardinal was handsome, intelligent, elegant, and licentious. He was also ambitious to become prime minister.

To become prime minister, Cardinal Rohan needed the Queen's friendship and backing. He had alienated her some ten years previously, when he ridiculed the Austrian Court of Empress Maria Theresa, mother of Marie Antoinette. Marie had never spoken to Rohan after that, although he did everything in his power to repair the breach.

Naturally the Cardinal listened attentively when Jeanne told him the Queen wanted the diamond necklace badly but didn't want the King to know about it as she had spent so much money on jewelry. Jeanne proposed that he buy the necklace as a favor for Marie, and the Queen could repay him in installments which the King wouldn't notice. As a "confidante of the Queen," Jeanne promised to arrange everything, and the eager Cardinal took the bait.

But Jeanne's fertile mind had already worked out a plan for getting not only the fee for the sale of the necklace, but the necklace itself. To do this she would need the services of confederates, including a forger her husband knew. So she went back home, told her husband la Motte of her plans, and enlisted the aid of his forger friend, Marc Antoine Rétaux de Villette. The men left their army posts and returned to Paris with Jeanne.

Meanwhile, the Cardinal became more and more involved with the beautiful go-between and lavished gifts on her, including a beautiful house in Versailles. When he complained her plans were developing too slowly, Jeanne told the Cardinal that she had a secret appointment with the Queen one night in the royal gardens—the Grove of Venus—at Versailles and invited him to eavesdrop. He peered through the bushes while Jeanne met in the dark with a young prostitute who was hired to take the part of the Queen. Any doubts the Cardinal might have had were dissipated.

The next step was to get correspondence started between Cardinal Rohan and "Marie Antoinette," with the aid of the forger Villette. Although the "Queen" would not allow Cardinal Rohan to visit her at the Palace, she agreed to the acquisition of the jewel. The Cardinal drew up the contract to purchase the necklace for 1,600,000 francs, to be paid at the rate of 400,000 francs each six months, with interest to be added to each payment.

The contract was signed by Cardinal Rohan, the jewelers, and afterward the forger wrote "approved" by each paragraph and signed "Marie Antoinette of France" at the bottom of each page. The Cardinal then asked the jewelers to bring the necklace to his home. He showed them the fully approved contract, which they copied, and they left the jewel case with Rohan.

The next night the Cardinal and his valet took the case to Jeanne's apartment in Versailles. Both hid as a cloaked messenger arrived and took possession of the necklace "In the name of the Queen." Shortly after the Cardinal and his valet left, so did Count la Motte and the necklace—to England.

Bessenger and Böhmer gladly paid Jeanne the 200,000 francs for her efforts in negotiating the sale.

When the first payment came due, Jeanne gave 30,000 francs to the Cardinal for the interest payment but said the Queen had asked for a three-month delay on the payment on the principal.

The jewelers became very upset over the delay and wrote a letter to the Queen. She, understandably enough, didn't know what they were writing about. "This Böhmer must certainly be mad," she said as she burned the letter. When they received no reply, the jewelers, who were being hounded by their own creditors, went to see the Queen.

After what must have been a tempestuous scene, the angry Queen agreed to call in Cardinal Rohan for an explanation. So the poor Cardinal, after waiting ten years to get an audience with Queen Marie, finally got it—but under what circumstances! Realizing at last that he had been duped by his beautiful mistress, he told the Queen that the necklace must be in Jeanne's possession.

Furious, the Queen demanded the King arrest the Cardinal. Rohan was thrown in the Bastille, together with Jeanne, Villette, and as many of her confederates as could be seized.

The trial began May 22, 1786, before sixty-four judges and following nine months of interrogation in the Bastille. One of the first points brought out was the forged signatures of the Queen. The Royal Family used only their given names; never could it be "Marie Antoinette of France." How this got by an experienced man like Rohan cannot be explained.

A few of the conspirators were freed. Some, including Villette, who was proven to be the cloaked messenger, were exiled. A crowd hostile to the Royal Family clamored for the freedom of the Cardinal, which would make the hated Marie Antoinette seem guilty; the judges gave him his freedom at the price of giving up his offices and titles and revenues. The Cardinal retired to his estates in Germany and spent his remaining years in charitable works connected with his church. He died in 1803. The absent Count de la Motte was sentenced to flogging, branding, and life imprisonment, and loss of all his goods to the King. But he was safe in England.

Jeanne was beaten and flogged, naked, in the courtyard of the Palais de Justice, then was branded with a hot iron on both shoulders with a "V" sign for *voleuse* ("thief"). She was sentenced for life to the house of correction for females, the Salpêtrière Prison, and all her goods were forfeited to the King. She could have followed her husband to England, but apparently she felt it proved her "innocence" to stay put.

In 1787, she escaped. She wrote the story of her life and had it published. In it she charged the Cardinal had been the one who obtained the necklace for the Queen and had been her lover. The Queen's reputation, none the best at the time, took a bad jolting at Jeanne's hands. At a time when the French people were ready for revolt, the public was only too glad to believe anything detrimental to Marie.

Had the Cardinal been acquitted, Jeanne's personal vendetta would have been useless. But the judgment handed down, while sparing his life, presumed his guilt. The story of the necklace, involving huge amounts of money and the Queen's secret trysts, fed scandals that were to lead to revolution. Tallyrand had warned, "Watch out for this diamond necklace business. It may well rock the throne of France."

The Queen undoubtedly had been guilty of secret affairs and bad judgment. The Cardinal had a great deal to answer for, too. It is ironic that neither was guilty of misbehavior in their dealings with the jewels, but it was in fact the necklace that proved the catalyst of their undoing.

Mirabeau wrote: "Madame de la Motte's voice alone brought on the horrors of July 14th [Bastille Day], 1789, and October fifth [the Women's March on Versailles]." The last resulted in the Royal Family being taken under guard to the Tuileries in Paris.

Jeanne died in an orgy in London in 1791. Marie Antoinette was guillotined on October 16, 1793, at age thirty-eight. Napoleon had stated, "The Queen's death must be dated from the Diamond Necklace trial."

The necklace was broken up and the diamonds scattered. The Duchess of Sutherland is reputed to own twenty-two of them, and the Duke of Dorset had some of the diamonds set in a diadem. Jim Brady bought one of the four large tassels for Lillian Russell.

The family of the impoverished Cardinal considered the price of the necklace a debt of honor, and, over a period of more than 100 years, they paid every cent to the jewelers and their heirs.

6

The Light of Peace

*Because of the rarity and unique qualities of the diamond it should
stand for the highest aspirations and achievements of mankind.*
—M. B. Zale, co-founder of the Zale Corporation

In contrast to the Queen's Necklace, which brought out
the worst in man, there is another diamond which is
dedicated to peace and the uplifting of the human spirit
through support of worthy endeavors. The gem is beautifully named "the Light of Peace."

A few years ago when I learned through the always
active jewelers' grapevine that a huge diamond had been
purchased for a purpose other than profit, I was both
dubious and delighted. In my long association with the
jewelry business, I had never heard of such a thing. It was
difficult to believe that one of the largest and finest
diamonds ever found was to be used for such an un-
worldly and noncommercial purpose. But when I learned
that the owner was the Zale Corporation, the world's
largest jewelry firm, I knew that this was no mere publicity
stunt. Since Zale is noted for its philanthropies, it was
obvious this diamond was to have a unique place in
history and was not going to be lost as the private treasure
of a few individuals, or buried in a museum.

Leo Fields at Zale's headquarters arranged for me to
see the stone, which was kept under elaborate guard.

For the uninitiated, the stone would have been unim-
pressive. It was still the way it had been found, with a
nondescript coat of ferrous oxide that indicated its alluvial
source. Nothing of its potential beauty was visible. I was
told that it weighed 434.60 carats. It was by far the largest
diamond that I had ever held in my hand, and I admit it

The Light of Peace, a 435-carat rough diamond, is shown here with 28 carats of rough diamonds on the left and 30.8 carats of cut diamonds on the right. Credit: The Zale Corporation

gave me quite a thrill. Four hundred and thirty-five carats! Since there are 142 carats to the avoirdupois ounce, 435 carats would add up to a fraction over three ounces. Diamonds that size are not come by every day.

I asked where it had been found and was disappointed to learn that it had been purchased on the open market in Antwerp and that it had been discovered "somewhere" in West Africa. Wasn't there a more exciting story about its origin? The Company did not give out any other details.

I stayed an extra day in New York to observe the start of the removal of the oxide coat. It was a not particularly glamorous operation, and only the knowledge that a stone of fabulous value was being worked on made it exciting. A quantity of acid was placed over a gas flame and presently the acid began to bubble. That's all there was to it, but many more steps lay ahead before the gem's beauty would be revealed. I left for home with the thought that I had had an intimate view of the stone at one of its starting points.

My guess is that the stone was discovered in Sierra Leone, the source of a few very large and very fine diamonds. Allen Ginsberg, president of Zale's International Diamond Division, who personally showed me the stone, told me the diamond would prove to have an excellent white color, which is another reason for believing its origins are in Sierra Leone. Diamonds from that country are noted for exceptionally fine color.

The circumstances of its discovery can only be imagined. In all possibility, it was found by a native worker. Let's assume this worker hadn't had much luck lately, but suddenly he saw the lump in a bed of muck. Quickly he picked it up and rubbed the mud off the stone. It was heavy for its size, and he had a fleeting thought that this was, indeed, the giant diamond he had always dreamed of finding. Still, he couldn't be sure.

Very excited, he hurried to the overseer to report the find. The overseer would have recognized it for a diamond immediately, except for its size. Only twice before had a diamond larger than 435 carats been found in Sierra Leone up to that time (1969), and the foreman had never seen a diamond that large in all his years of diamond mining. He could well have refused to believe his eyes. But, of course, it was a diamond. The worker received a large reward for finding it, which could keep him for the rest of his life, provided, of course, that he avoided the gaming tables and other pleasures which always are at hand to lighten the burden of miners' lives and pockets.

Subsequently, through the ordinary channels, the diamond found its way to the bourse in Antwerp.

In all recorded history, fewer than fifty gem diamonds weighed over 400 carats when found. The Light of Peace is possibly the eighteenth largest rough gem diamond ever discovered whose history is known, although some records show there were about fifteen others which were larger, but whose whereabouts and ultimate disposition remain unknown, probably forever.

The Zale rough diamond made its formal American

debut on January 14, 1970. Cleaned of its oxide coating, the stone was a beautiful sight even before it was cut and polished.

The showing, held in the board room of the Manufacturers Hanover Trust Company on Park Avenue, was attended by the principals of the Zale Corporation, officers of the bank, and representatives of the media. I was happy to be among those present.

Zale's president, Ben Lipshy, who became chairman of the board, said in announcing the Company's plans for the diamond:

"We held the stone for several months before announcing it. Though we were anxious to share the news of our acquisition with the world, we somehow felt a burden of responsibility. A responsibility that prevented us from flaunting the stone. If we had acquired our diamond at another moment in history, there might be no 'burden of ownership.' At least, it wouldn't seem so apparent to us. But, in the light of the restlessness of the world—the turmoil that seems to have worked its way into every corner of the earth—how should we present such a magnificent find? We felt the best way to share the indescribable beauty of this diamond was to dedicate it to peace.

"Our conviction and dedication to the cause of peace is quite real. And we wanted to emphasize that conviction by more than simply naming this large diamond 'Light of Peace.' We have made a commitment that encompasses a special fund, and a permanent mounting for the Light of Peace in a work of art."

Morris B. Zale, co-founder who now is chairman of the executive committee, said: "We felt that it was time for private industry to begin taking a more active role in promoting peace which has up to now been essentially a governmental function.

"If nothing else, we hope that this step will inspire other industries to take a more active role in helping the cause of peace for the protection of world trade and as a contribution to humanity."

News of the Zale acquisition spread quickly. *The New*

York Times, in a front page story, showed a picture of the diamond alongside a ruler which showed its two-inch length. In a lengthy article, the *Times* described the six armed guards who stood stiffly at attention near the glass case where the diamond lay. The article even described the proposed cutting plans in detail. Clearly, the *Times* was impressed.

Newsweek added an interesting sidelight in describing the arrival of the diamond from Antwerp. Entitled "A Stone for Janet" and showing the diamond in full size, the article went on:

"Winging across the Atlantic in a load of airmail, the registered package seemed innocuous enough; the size of

The Light of Peace diamond, shown actual size, is remarkable for the purity of its color and its brilliance. The 130.27-carat stone is probably the largest cut American diamond. The Hope diamond, for comparison, is 44.5 carats. Credit: The Zale Corporation

a cigar box, it was carefully wrapped, well tied with string and addressed to the Zale Corp., New York City. But appearances were deceptive. The package was met at the airport by an armored truck; then it was tagged 'For Janet—Personal' and sequestered in a double vault—until last week when its contents were finally put on display. And that was done with a bit of flourish, since the package contained a 435-carat diamond, one of the largest ever found."

The article explained that the largest stone cut from the diamond would be called the Light of Peace and would have a value of up to $5,000,000. Then the article asked: "And who is Janet? She is Morris Zale's 7-year-old grand-daughter, and she hasn't even seen the Light of Peace. 'I told Janet to make her father give it to her,' said Grandpa Zale, 'but she doesn't want it. She'd rather have an ice cream cone!' "

The world press was generous in its stories of the stone and its purpose.

The diamond was shown at the fashionable Diamond Ball in New York a few days later and attracted enormous interest. The ball is given each year for the benefit of worthy causes. This time it was to aid the Institute of International Education. The Light of Peace was off to a fine start.

After weeks of study, work started on cutting the stone. There are two methods of dividing a rough diamond, cleaving and sawing, the stone itself usually dictating the best method. In this case, both sawing and cleaving followed.

After first sawing the back of the diamond, an operation requiring six weeks, a piece weighing 47.80 carats was then cleaved and fashioned into two marquise stones, each weighing over 9 carats. Further cutting and cleaving produced ten other satellite diamonds of different shapes. They weighed from 6.93 carats down to 0.37.

The principal diamond, a pear-shaped stone which was designated as the name stone, weighs 130.27 carats. In all, the finished diamonds equaled 172.83 carats and the loss in cutting was a staggering, but not unexpected, 262.77 carats.

Owing to the magnitude of the Light of Peace rough, special cutting equipment was brought in from Belgium. It took from January 1970 to October 1971 to complete the cutting of the stones. All work was done in the company's New York cutting plant.

I was privileged to witness the unveiling of the finished diamond in New York on November 2, 1972. Donald Zale, as company president, presided at the affair. He stated that the permanent setting for the great diamond was sculptured by Ben Zvi, the renowned artisan from Israel, who calls his work "the family of man linked together by holding each other." The diamond revolved in a beam of light, and the impact it made on the group assembled for the dedication can only be described as awesome. The Light of Peace has to be one of the most beautiful and brilliant of the great diamonds.

It is the second largest pear-shaped diamond in the world, bowing only to the Cullinan I. The white color has no trace of off-color tint. The cutting gives it truly unusual brilliancy. In size, it rates eleventh among the known and authenticated cut diamonds of the world, although there are thirteen others believed to be larger, but whose identities have been lost. It is the largest diamond ever cut in the United States and it has the added distinction of being the largest cut diamond in the U. S. A. Also, it is the largest cut anywhere since the Cullinans in 1908. The Light of Peace is judged by some authorities as being the largest of its fine quality in the world.

Mrs. Lyndon B. Johnson and Dr. William McGill of Columbia University co-chaired a distinguished body known as the Zale Award Committee. The Zale Foundation pledged $750,000 for the committee's use. An annual award of $25,000 is made to an American "to honor timely and significant contributions to the betterment of mankind." In addition, each winner receives a casting of the sculpture which holds the diamond, plus a replica of the Light of Peace in the setting to represent the spirit of the award.

The committee determines some field of endeavor —such as education, health research, civil rights, ecology—from which the recipient of the award is selected. The Light of Peace diamond is to be under the committee's control for ten years, during which it will determine how the gem will be exhibited to raise funds to further the work of each year's award winner. For example, if the recipient is selected for his work in environmental preservation, the funds generated by the diamond that year will be used to support further work in that field.

Mrs. Johnson, in an interview before the unveiling, stressed that the committee would act autonomously and independently. She added: "We will develop our own procedures, and make our own decisions and selections."

Can you think of a more noble way in which to utilize the beauty and fascination of a great diamond?

7

Where Diamonds Come From

Up above the world so high,
Like a diamond in the sky.
—Old nursery rhyme

The origin of diamonds remains shrouded in mystery, although we can make some educated guesses. One ancient theory which persisted for centuries is that they rained down from the sky. Until the finding of diamonds in underground deposits called kimberlite pipes in South Africa in 1870, all these precious stones had been located on the surface, which probably gave rise to the old tales.

Not too long ago, radiotelescope observations indicated that some of the vast dust clouds in space may contain great quantities of very tiny grains of carbon. Since carbon is the diamond's basic ingredient, there may in effect be diamonds in dust clouds out in space.

The Smithsonian Center for Short-Lived Phenomena recently confirmed that a rare type of meteorite which fell in Finland contained traces of diamonds. They were microscopic and worthless, like those described in the dust clouds, but diamonds nonetheless.

The theory of the meteorite diamonds is that they were formed in outer space when their parent planet collided with another and broke into cosmic debris. So far our astronauts have found no evidence of diamonds on the moon. While some authorities scoff at any such possibility, each time rock samples are returned from a trip to the moon the question about moon diamonds is asked.

The generally accepted theory of the creation of diamonds is that they were formed many millions of years

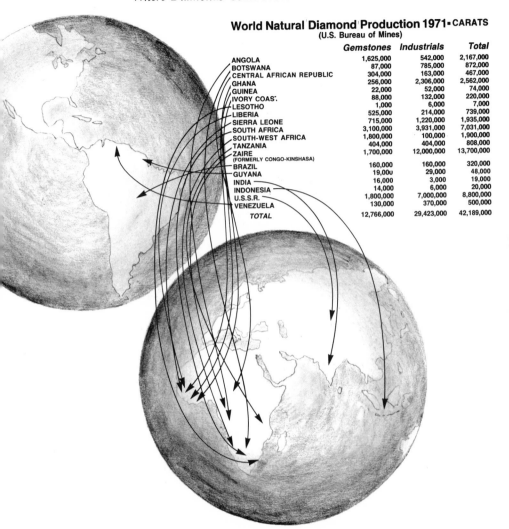

World Natural Diamond Production 1971 ▪ CARATS
(U.S. Bureau of Mines)

	Gemstones	Industrials	Total
ANGOLA	1,625,000	542,000	2,167,000
BOTSWANA	87,000	785,000	872,000
CENTRAL AFRICAN REPUBLIC	304,000	163,000	467,000
GHANA	256,000	2,306,000	2,562,000
GUINEA	22,000	52,000	74,000
IVORY COAST.	88,000	132,000	220,000
LESOTHO	1,000	6,000	7,000
LIBERIA	525,000	214,000	739,000
SIERRA LEONE	715,000	1,220,000	1,935,000
SOUTH AFRICA	3,100,000	3,931,000	7,031,000
SOUTH-WEST AFRICA	1,800,000	100,000	1,900,000
TANZANIA	404,000	404,000	808,000
ZAIRE (FORMERLY CONGO-KINSHASA)	1,700,000	12,000,000	13,700,000
BRAZIL	160,000	160,000	320,000
GUYANA	19,000	29,000	48,000
INDIA	16,000	3,000	19,000
INDONESIA	14,000	6,000	20,000
U.S.S.R.	1,800,000	7,000,000	8,800,000
VENEZUELA	130,000	370,000	500,000
TOTAL	12,766,000	29,423,000	42,189,000

Where diamonds originate. Credit: U.S. Bureau of Mines. Artist: Joe Barros.

ago when carbon was subjected to enormous heat and pressure miles below the earth's surface.

An exciting breakthrough in diamond dating was recently announced by U. S. scientists, who found that there are considerable differences in the age of diamonds. Some diamonds contain inclusions of argon gas formed at

Diamonds were formed under tremendous heat and pressure when the world was young. Credit: DeBeers Consolidated Diamond Mines, Ltd.

the same time the stones solidified. The age of this gas can be determined with complex instruments.

These tests indicated diamonds from South Africa's Premier Mine "are at least 800,000,000 years old." Diamonds from some other South African mines date back to "only 140,000,000 years." The age of diamonds has been a puzzle for years, but it looks like scientists will soon have some answers.

The theory that diamonds were formed under great heat and pressure is corroborated by the fact that synthetic diamonds have been formed under temperatures approximating 5000 degrees Fahrenheit (ordinary iron melts at around 2790 degrees), with pressures of 1,000,000 pounds per square inch. In nature, this could have happened only in a suitable molten rock material in the earth's interior.

Internal pressures caused cracks in the overlying rock formations. The molten magma was forced upward into the cracks, gradually cooling as it moved away from its original mass. Some of it rose to the surface of the earth in fiery volcanic eruptions. In cooling, the magma formed basic igneous rock. Kimberlite, the only known source rock of diamonds, is igneous rock, although much of it has deteriorated into a characteristic blue clay.

Some of these eruptions formed volcanoes. But everywhere that the molten rock reached the surface it also congealed in a tube or "pipe" of igneous rock extending deep down through the earth's crust. These pipes, which may be hundreds of feet in diameter, are the "mother lodes" of diamonds, the matrix in which nature cast these most precious of gemstones.

In the passage of millions of years, the surface of the earth was changed drastically by repeated upheavals, the slow but relentless erosion caused by torrential rains, changes of temperature, the abrasion of wind-borne sand, the gouging of rivers and glaciers. Volcanic peaks were worn down to the level of the plains, their rock reduced to sand and carried away to distant seas. Geologists tell us there were a series of upheavals through eons of time, each followed by the inevitable leveling process.

Gradually the diamonds in their beds were uncovered. Ancient rivers and glacial ice carried them far from their original sources. Some were buried anew in stream beds. Others were washed into the sea and covered by millions and billions of tons of sand or debris, some were swept back by the waves onto newly created beaches. The courses of rivers changed. New mountain ranges rose from later eruptions. Land masses emerged from the sea or were engulfed by the waters. The faces of the continents changed. Such was the action of natural erosive forces which leveled the mountains containing the diamonds, that tremendous amounts of them are found in alluvial deposits.

The diamonds survived this merciless battering and were scattered to many areas. In some cases, such as in South Africa, the roots of prehistoric volcanoes remain. These are the channels through which the molten rock surged to the surface. The mountain peaks have disappeared, but the channels still reach down into the earth.

Within them is the kimberlite. In some cases they are seeded with diamonds. There are many hundreds of kimberlite pipes which have no trace of diamonds. However, diamond-bearing pipes are probably where all diamonds originally came from once they reached the earth's surface.

The earliest records of diamonds go back to about 800 B. C. to the stones found in India, for many years the only known source. These were found along the courses of ancient rivers. By 700 B. C., the gravel beds were being combed systematically for diamonds by many thousands of laborers. Their trading center, Golconda, lay within a few miles of the modern city of Hyderabad. From Golconda, traders carried the diamonds to Rome and Greece and east to China.

The great Indian diamond beds finally became exhausted around the end of the seventeenth century, and until just the past few years no efforts were made to explore for new possibilities. Today India is producing diamonds again. Each year it shows a steady gain and

Golconda, The Diamond Trading Center of India in the 1600s. Credit: N. W. Ayer & Son, Inc.

there is hope that the country will be a major factor once more.

The next diamond discovery of major proportions took place in Brazil, in the state of Minas Gerais, in 1726, shortly after the Indian sources gave out. Gold prospectors found by sheer chance that the pebbles they were using for tallies in their gambling games were, in fact, diamonds and far more valuable than the minerals they were seeking.

The news of Brazil's great find was received with incredulity and consternation in Europe. Those who owned Indian diamonds feared that their values would

The Brazilian alluvial diamond site on the Jequitinhonha River. Credit: Mrs. Eunice Miles, Gemological Institute of America

decrease. Rumors were spread to the effect that the Brazilian stones were soft and very inferior to those of India. The false rumors brought the sale of Brazilian diamonds to a standstill. Portuguese traders then shipped Brazilian diamonds to Goa, their colony on the southwestern coast of India, and from there they went out as products of India. It was years before the diamonds from South America found favor.

Actually, Brazilian diamonds are of excellent quality and color and as good as those from other countries. When my wife and I visited that country some years ago, I had the opportunity of examining huge parcels of their finest diamonds from Minas Gerais. Most of these gems were as fine as I have ever seen.

Brazil's mines, after producing millions of carats, passed their peak by the middle of the nineteenth century, and the world had lost its second great source. Recent attempts at restoring production have been moderately successful.

The world was not to be without a major diamond source for long, however, and what took place changed the entire picture of diamonds.

It all started inauspiciously enough in 1866 near Hopetown, South Africa. One day, the children of a Boer farmer named Jacobs picked up a pretty bright pebble and took it home to show. A neighbor, one Van Niekirk, was shown the pebble, and he offered to buy it. Mrs. Jacobs, who was sure her children could pick up such pebbles at will, readily gave it to him.

Van Niekirk wasn't sure what he had. He offered it for sale to several traders, but none showed any interest until a hunter and trader named O'Reilly bought it for a trifle. He had a vague notion that it might be a diamond, so he took it to a Dr. W. Atherstone, a mineralogist.

Dr. Atherstone made tests and determined the stone to be a diamond. It weighed 21 carats, and a value of $2500 was placed on it in its uncut form. Named the "Eureka," it later was placed in the gavel of the Premier of South Africa.

When the news reached London, diamond dealers passed it off as a freak find. They couldn't have been more wrong. However, three years passed before a second diamond was found near Hopetown. The same Van Niekirk heard about it and traded a considerable number of cattle for it. This stone weighed 83 carats and brought Van Niekirk $50,000, an incredible sum for him. Within another year or two, diamonds were being found in exciting quantities. Fortune hunters rushed into the Vaal River valley—and the greatest diamond rush the world has known was on.

The first of the South African pipes to be discovered was the famous Jagersfontein in 1870, although it was not realized then that kimberlite was the major source of all diamonds which had reached the surface. The Jagersfontein was followed in rapid succession by other pipe discoveries. Only then did geologists realize that these volcanic pipes were the true original source of these diamonds.

In the following two decades, four more highly productive mines were discovered: the Dutoitspan, Bultfontein, DeBeers, and Kimberley. In 1891, prospectors struck it rich at the Wesselton mine, and soon after the tremendous Premier mine near Pretoria was discovered by Sir Thomas Cullinan. Searching for diamond-bearing gravel, he found some small stones while prospecting in a stream bed. Studying the area, he reached the conclusion that the diamonds had been washed down from a nearby property owned by Joachim Prinsloo.

Prinsloo, with a reputation for being hostile toward diamond prospectors, always carried his rifle with him. He refused to sell his land and allowed no stranger on his property. Sir Thomas, who was just plain Thomas at the time, proved to be no exception. Some sources say Cullinan finally bought the property for $125,000 after repeated matching of wits with Prinsloo. Others have it that he waited until Prinsloo died and then purchased the land from his daughter. This seems more reasonable. At any rate, Cullinan's deductions were right. He found a kimber-

An aerial view of South Africa's most famous mine, the Premier, showing its "Big Hole." Credit: N. W. Ayer & Son, Inc.

lite pipe and the Premier became one of South Africa's most famous mines. When the world's largest and greatest diamond was found there in 1905, it was named the Cullinan.

If South Africa had diamonds, why wouldn't they be found in adjacent lands? These countries were undeveloped and exploration was slow. But, one by one, rich new fields were discovered. Diamonds were found in Southwest Africa in 1908. The Republic of the Congo (Zäire), presently the largest producer, yielded its first diamonds in 1916, but only five percent of its output is suitable for gems; the rest is industrial quality. Angola, next door, has diamond-bearing areas that are really a continuation of the Congo's, but, in amazing contrast, their diamonds average more than half gem quality, which is far above the world average.

Diamonds were found in the Gold Coast, now Ghana, in 1919. Sierra Leone deposits were discovered in 1930, and, while the majority of their output is industrial quality, their gemstones are noted for size and excellent quality. The largest diamond ever taken from an alluvial deposit was found in Sierra Leone. Called the Woyie River diamond, it weighed a fabulous 770 carats.

This area has produced diamonds of 530 and 250 carats and many weighing more than 50 carats. And as this is being written comes the news that a diamond weighing 968.90 carats has just been found there. It is the third largest ever found anywhere and has been named Star of Sierra Leone.

In Tanzania (then Tanganyika), unimportant finds had been made as early as 1910. A Canadian geologist, Dr. John T. Williamson, became convinced that huge deposits lay hidden in eastern Africa. He spent five years in a systematic search of Tanzania, all but exhausting his financial resources. Then in 1940 at Mwadui, about 100 miles south of Lake Victoria, Dr. Williamson's faith was rewarded by the discovery of an incredibly rich pipe mine. In area over 360 acres, it is one of the world's largest. The output runs to eighty percent gem quality in contrast to the pipe mine average of 20 percent gem. Many unusually fine stones have been taken from this mine. The best known is a pink diamond which weighed 54 carats. It was cut to yield a gem of 23.5 carats, which Dr. Williamson presented to Queen Elizabeth II as a wedding gift. Although it is relatively small as famous diamonds go, it is one of the most valuable.

Some time ago in a New York cutter's stock, I was shown an exquisite 19-carat pink diamond from the same mine. With a most unusual and beautiful tint, it compares favorably with the Queen's pink jewel.

In South Africa, no major discoveries were made from 1902, when the Premier was found, until 1960. While

The newest diamond mine—the Finsch mine in South Africa—was opened officially in 1967. The Finsch is being worked by the "open pit method." Credit: N. W. Ayer & Son, Inc.

searching for asbestos on his property, Allister Fincham chanced upon two clues—pyrope garnets and thick vegetation. Further investigation showed he had located a kimberlite pipe. Fincham now had to make an important decision. He had spent two years proving payable asbestos deposits and was at the point of starting to mine. Should he drop the asbestos venture, which now looked like a sure thing, and risk everything to prove a kimberlite pipe which, after all, might not contain diamonds in payable quantities?

He would have to form a new company, raise funds, sink test holes, dig prospecting pits and trenches, and, above all, find water to work the project. However, he, like many another before him, was gripped by diamond fever—and asbestos was forgotten. The Finsch mine, as it was named, has proven very successful. DeBeers purchased it from the Finsch interests in 1963.

Of the hundreds of kimberlite pipes found, only a few have yielded many diamonds. Some mines have produced diamonds on a paying basis for only a few years before they petered out. Some never were profitable from the start. Diamonds occur less frequently as depth increases, so a mine has a finite life. The fact that the best paying part of the mine is at the upper levels can well lead us to believe that when the tops of the volcanoes were weathered and scattered, possibly the greatest part of the diamond deposits went with the action.

The world-famous Kimberley mine, which closed in 1914, produced 14,500,000 carats of diamonds. Now it remains a water-filled hole, affectionately called "The Big Hole." More recently the famous Jagersfontein mine has ceased operations.

The history of diamond production, like most mining, is one of discovery, depletion, and new discoveries made possible by continuous search. Diamonds have been found in Botswana, just north of the Republic of South Africa, in recent years—100 years after the discovery of diamonds in Kimberley. The Botswana property includes the Orapa pipe, second only to the Williamson in size. Although production is expected to be largely industrial quality, it should prove profitable, as there is little overburden to be removed. Botswana hopes to gain financial independence from her diamonds eventually.

Other African nations are pressing the search for diamonds. The Ivory Coast is not a very large producer but accounts for as many gems as industrial stones. Ghana, next door, produces more than three times the yield of the Ivory Coast in gem quality and is a very large supplier of industrials. Guinea is still one of the smaller producers in Africa, but Lesotho, formerly Basutoland, made the headlines in 1967 when a 601.25-carat stone was found there by Ernestine Ramaboa, wife of the owner of a

Petrus Ramaboa proudly holds the Lesotho diamond, a 601.25-carat stone, which his wife found on their thirty-foot-square claim.

tiny, thirty-foot square claim. She and her husband, Petrus, had worked hard on his claim for five years, averaging less than a dollar a day with tiny stones until she came across the "big" diamond, large as an egg. Ramaboa put the diamond in his pocket, and he and Ernestine walked and hitchhiked 110 miles to the capital, Maseru, where they sold it for over $300,000.

There are presently great hopes for diamond production in Venezuela. In 1970, that nation surpassed Brazil, producing almost 500,000 carats, of which two-thirds were gem quality. Exploitation of Venezuela's alluvial resources is hampered by natural barriers. One of the latest discoveries was in the jungles near 3200-foot Angel Falls, the world's highest. The area of this strike is almost inaccessible except by small planes, helicopters, and canoes.

Next door to Venezuela lies Guyana, formerly British Guiana, which supplies a very limited quantity of diamonds. Considering that both these countries border Brazil, and remembering Brazil's history, the search for new fields goes on continually.

Meanwhile, the South African fields, far from playing out, appear to be producing new finds. For many years there has been a theory that a possible 3,000,000,000 carats of diamonds were lost when the terrain of Kimberley was eroded to its present level.

An article in *International Diamonds*, Number 2 (1972), states that it is estimated that millions of years ago Kimberley was 5000 feet high and that, in the process of nature's leveling, the 3,000,000,000 carats which were thought to be originally in Kimberley's volcanic peaks have been scattered. One item stressed is that the Orange River, which has given up so many diamonds, has not been so generous with its yield after the river drops a precipitous 492 feet into a canyon, along which it flows through mountain ranges until it emerges onto a plain thirty-one miles from the sea. For several decades, there has been no record of diamonds found in payable quantities below the falls to the sea.

The article pursues a theory that the ancient river channels have changed direction during the ages, and geologists are exploring this possibility.

One of the two companies mentioned engaged in this exploration is Baken Diamante, a subsidiary of the Canadian–South African Diamond Corporation, Ltd., based in Vancouver, British Columbia. Two of its engineers, R. Baxter-Brown and H. Jenner-Clarke, have spent years following the theory of the river's changed courses. *International Diamonds* mentions that R. Baxter-Brown found the first diamond after he deepened a trench to reach one of the fossil channels. It was termed a "historic find."

The Canadian company, which owns mining rights in

Two views of the operations of the Canadian–South Africa Diamond Corporation, Ltd. Credit: Ronald V. Markham

South Africa, South West Africa, and other countries, has reported discoveries of three alluvial diamond beds along the Orange River by following the theory that the river changed its course. The old beds are being traced and the old gravels located under the overlaying calcrete foundation.

In addition to the alluvial discoveries, the firm has also located a number of kimberlite pipes, including one which measures a mile by a mile and a half at its surface, which would make it the largest in the world. It is not yet known if these pipes are diamondiferous or, if they are, whether they will prove to be payable. A full evaluation of their potential is awaited. The Canadian syndicate is headed by Ronald V. Markham.

Diamonds under the Seas

A British engineer named Peter Keeble had a theory that huge quantities of diamonds could be found off the mouth of the Orange River on the west coast of South Africa. He thought that possibly this deposit came from undersea volcanic action and not as a result of deposits by the river. In 1939, he managed to bring up a few diamonds of high quality, but he couldn't find anyone willing to back him financially. However, he was able to form a company that purchased rights to a large offshore area. A few more diamonds were recovered, but a suitable process for dredging the bottom could not be devised, so the project was abandoned while he returned to Britain to serve during World War II.

Collins' first diamond dredge, Barge 77. Credit: Jewelers Circular-Keystone

After the war, he went from one financier to another in an attempt to raise money to work the ocean floor. At every turn he was told his ideas were impractical. Finally he was advised to get in touch with a Texas oil production engineer named Sam Collins, who lived in England at that time. Collins felt he could solve the many technical problems.

Together, they managed to get capital enough to purchase the offshore rights from Keeble's former associates. Then Collins designed a 160-foot barge equipped with dredging machinery which he had built at Durban, South Africa. They christened it Barge 77. It was an awkward-looking, top-heavy vessel. Durban authorities doubted its seaworthiness and refused it permission to leave the dock. But one dark night, Keeble had the barge towed out of port and to the mouth of the Orange River.

Keeble and Collins soon recovered many diamonds, all of gem quality, and had a second barge built in anticipation of producing as many as 1,000,000 carats a year. Their success fired the imagination of others, and a hysterical rush resulted for concession areas off the Southwest African and Namaqualand coasts.

Collins eventually put together a fleet of a dozen ships at a cost of more than $5,000,000. The diamonds recovered did not justify his optimism: Barge 77 foundered, and he found himself badly overextended. In due course, he allied his company with DeBeers, which had the organization to pursue the operation on a more realistic level. So far, sea mining has not proven to be the bonanza antici-

A huge diamond dredge, the Pomona, showing the hoses going over the barge's bow at deck level. Credit: The Anglo-American Corporation of S.A., Ltd.

Diamonds from the sea: Mining off the southwest coast of Africa. This barge dredges up diamond-bearing gravel and silt from the ocean floor. The barge is its own floating treatment plant. Credit: N. W. Ayer & Son, Inc.

pated by the two men who originated the idea. It is hoped, though, that in time it will prove a substantial addition to other diamond sources.

Diamonds in the Sand

One of the most valuable pieces of real estate on earth is a narrow strip of forbidding desert coastline starting from the mouth of the Orange River, which separates South Africa and South West Africa, and extending north for sixty miles along the Atlantic.

Owned by the Consolidated Mines of South West Africa, Ltd., a member of the DeBeers group, these coastal sands are among the largest producers of gem diamonds in the world. In fact, this stretch of coast is aptly called "the Richest Sands on Earth." Since 1956, the area has yielded about 1,000,000 carats of diamonds annually; but,

An aerial view of the Marine Diamond Corporation's beach-mining operations on the southwestern African coast. Credit: The Anglo-American Corporation of S.A., Ltd.

Plastic sheets cover sand supporting wall on the Southwest African coast as the diamond miners work toward the low-water mark on the beach. Credit: DeBeers Consolidated Diamond Mines, Ltd.

far more important, the stones are preponderately gem quality and, inexplicably, many of them are flawless.

The presence of diamonds along the coast was suspected 100 years ago, but no substantial finds were reported until 1908. The usual rush of miners followed. Many gems were recovered, but no one had any idea of the immense store of wealth which lay there until years later, when full recovery methods were developed.

What is the origin of these diamonds? One theory is that the diamonds were carried to the sea by prehistoric rivers from the tops of great inland pipes formed millions of years ago. The action of the waves probably concentrated the heavy stones on the beaches where they were buried by wind-blown sands.

Another long-standing theory is that the gems were carried landward from volcanic pipes in the depths of the sea. There are rocks at the bottom of the ocean in this territory similar to diamond-bearing kimberlite; many theorists hold that the diamonds found on the beaches and recovered from the sea are products of undersea volcanic activity.

Oddly, the diamonds found on the beaches and in the sea are as high as ninety-five percent gem quality. A test conducted by the Diamond Research Laboratory in Johannesburg a few years ago may explain the high ratio of gemstones.

In the test, six industrial quality stones from the Congo and Bakwanga and six gem diamonds from the South West African marine terraces were subjected to severe milling action. After only seven hours, all six of the low-quality diamonds had completely disappeared, while the total weight loss of the six gem diamonds, after 950 hours of milling, was found to be only 0.01 percent!

Undoubtedly, the diamonds in the present marine terraces were spread along the coast by waves which pounded them in a mass of gravel for a very long time. It is likely that this natural attrition mill disintegrated most of the physically weaker diamonds so that only the very sound stones remained.

Russia as a Diamond Source

Fearing the rise of Communism, the nations of the West, led by the U.S.A., forbade the sale of diamonds to Russia in the 1920s. After World War II, the Soviets needed them desperately for industrial expansion. How they developed their own sources makes interesting diamond lore.

In 1941, a Soviet geologist recommended that a thorough survey be made in Yakutia, in northern Siberia. The Soviets sent a large exploration party to the area. Members found nothing to make the terrible privations from the Arctic cold bearable. After two years, the explorers were rewarded by finding a few small diamonds. More important, they found pyrope garnets. But unlike Allister Fincham, who understood the significance of garnets in diamond discoveries—a knowledge which helped him to locate a mine in South Africa—the young Soviet geologists had no idea what they meant.

Back in Leningrad, two women who were interested in geological research had been following news of the exploring party with great interest. When they heard about the garnets they became quite excited. One of them, Larissa Popugaieva, volunteered for the 1954 expedition. The government permitted her to go along. Instead of looking for diamonds as all the others of the party did, she searched for pyrope garnets. Garnets don't always mean a diamond-bearing pipe is nearby. But she found garnets, and they led to the discovery of the first kimberlite pipe in Siberia. Subsequently her theory worked wonders, and Larissa, who had left her warm apartment in Leningrad for the freezing conditions of Yakutia, became immortalized in the history of Siberian development.

Many other pipes have been found in Siberia, a good proportion of them diamond-bearing. Of the twenty-five largest presently known diamond pipes, Siberia has twelve. The U.S.S.R. now claims to be the second largest diamond producer and predicts it will lead the world in another two or three years.

Scientists are pretty well agreed now that all the continents were joined at one time, so it is possible that new discoveries may be made in unexpected places. As a result of the great Siberian developments, Alaska and Canada must be considered possible sources of diamonds. The Antarctic, likewise, is considered a possible location.

As the world market for diamonds keeps expanding, it is interesting to see how nature reveals new hiding places to help production keep up with the demand.

8

A Visit to Kimberley

The rough diamond. The self-made man.
—Christie in *Evil Under the Sun*

Before I get into some of the more technical aspects of diamond mining, cutting, and distribution, come with me on a visit to fabled Kimberley, the South African city whose name is synonymous with diamonds. Anticipating the trip, I was extremely excited as our jetliner thundered down the runway of the Brussels airport, on take off, circled the city and headed south for faraway Africa.

For half a century the jewelry business had been my world and I had succumbed to the excitement of diamonds early in that period. I had bought and sold them, written and lectured about them, and had become immersed in the subject. Now my wife and I were actually on our way to visit the continent that had yielded some of the world's most famous gemstones.

Our brief stop in Kinshasa in the Congo (Zäire), with its famous river steaming in the background, was a good introduction to the continent, for the Congo is the world's greatest producer of diamonds. Its total almost equals the entire output of the rest of Africa. However, the Congo's diamonds are practically all industrial quality. Thanks to them, much of the world is able to afford the diamonds that contribute to the speed and precision of countless industrial processes.

A few days in Johannesburg gave us a chance to meet some officials of DeBeers Consolidated Mines, Ltd. A trip to Pretoria, one of South Africa's two capitals, afforded us the opportunity to visit the great Premier Mine, which has produced millions of carats of gem diamonds, including the Cullinan, by far the largest gem diamond ever found anywhere.

But it was not until we landed in Kimberley, a city of slightly more than 100,000 population on the flat African plain, that the world of diamonds began to unfold in earnest.

The Kimberley Club.

An officer of DeBeers Consolidated Mines, Ltd., Mr. J. Sandilands, met us at the tiny airport and escorted us to the famous Kimberley Club. Founded in 1881, diamond deals involving millions of dollars were formerly negotiated in the club's dark, wood-paneled bar and library. Everything about it was Victorian, from the heavy wooden furniture and paneled public rooms to the quietly efficient help in formal dark trousers and white coats. The visitors from America were treated like celebrities. In fact, we were told that the quarters assigned to us had been occupied by Queen Elizabeth II on her visit.

Next morning the century-old, highly respected English-language newspaper, the *Diamond Fields' Advertiser*, was delivered to our room. (Newspapers in South

Africa are printed either in English or Afrikaans.) A front page item headed "Distinguished U. S. Jeweler in City" led me to remark to my wife, "What do you know, there's another American jeweler in town." I then read on to learn that it was the Argenzios who were being referred to. What a nice way to be welcomed!

We were given a tour of the mines, viewing the vari-

The "Big Hole" at Kimberley, showing the shape of the diamond-bearing volcanic "pipe" that was one of the first diamond mines in South Africa. Kimberley was "mined out" in 1914, but in forty years of operation it produced 14,504,567 carats of diamonds. Credit: N. W. Ayer & Son, Inc.

ous processes whereby diamonds are separated from tons and tons of earth—a needle in a haystack operation—and then classified into the many grades from lowest industrial to most precious gemstone. The visit brought to life all the things that I had read about and had been fascinated by over the years. When I asked about security in the mines, a special performance of the famous DeBeers dogs was arranged for our benefit. Beautifully trained German shepherds on command scaled walls, leapt through fire, savagely attacked men who for the demonstration were wearing heavily padded protective gear, and then just as quickly retreated on command.

Perhaps the most impressive sight was the Big Hole, a yawning manmade crater near downtown Kimberley. This is what remains of the original Kimberley mine. Discovered in 1871, men labored for more than forty years to recover its treasure. In the process, they created a hole 1500 feet across and 3600 feet deep, excavating more than 25,000,000 tons of earth. This was a classic example of the kimberlite pipe, created in prehistoric times by molten lava forcing its way to the earth's surface from the fiercely hot interior.

The mine yielded more than 14,500,000 carats of diamonds—three tons—before it was exhausted in 1914. The mine's output was equivalent to almost half the world's annual production today. The crater is now fenced off for safety, but streets run around it and homes and office buildings are nearby. Vegetation has begun to grow on the precipitous upper slopes, and water has filled it to a depth of 700 feet. All in all, the abandoned Kimberley mine is as awesome a sight as a hole in the ground can be.

The diamond mining industry as we know it was born here. It all began with a party of prospectors led by a man with the rather exotic name of Fleetwood Rawstone. They pitched camp near the present site of Kimberley. When the cook, Damon, imbibed too generously and was unable to prepare the meals, Rawstone angrily sent him out to prospect seemingly barren ground as punishment. Much later, Damon came back, wild with excitement—and with several diamonds in his hands. Tables were overturned as Rawstone's men rushed off to stake out claims. Unfortunately for Rawstone, his claims proved worthless. But it proved a bonanza for others.

It soon became evident that here were diamonds in quantities never seen before. Prospectors flocked to the area, sleeping in shanties and tents set up beside ever-mounting piles of rubble. Property was in such demand that fortune seekers bought and sold claims only a few feet in area.

The miners were a tough and hearty lot who worked hard and played harder. One of their bars, the Diggers' Rest, has been reconstructed on the Kimberley Mine Museum site and is one of the city's attractions. There is a great deal of information about the pursuits and pleasures of the miners of the late 1800s, but not much about schools and churches.

Diamond mining in Kimberley in 1872. The claims were 31' × 31'. Credit: DeBeers Consolidated Diamond Mines, Ltd.

When the miners weren't working, fighting about claims, or drinking, they played tricks on each other. An often-told story is about a miner who liked to take one or another of the many girls of easy virtue to his shanty at night. One day when this miner was working on his claim, several of his buddies sawed the entire bottom of his shack. When the miner came home that night with his girl, his friends waited until they were sure that the propitious moment had arrived, then toppled the entire shack over.

Mining conditions were deplorable. There was little knowledge of mining techniques at first, and each man was out for himself, paying no regard to the rights of his neighbors. Eventually conditions became chaotic. The man most responsible for restoring order was Cecil John Rhodes.

Kimberley mining in 1875. When the roadways collapsed, bucket pulleys brought diamond dirt to the miners. Credit: DeBeers Consolidated Diamond Mines, Ltd.

Cecil Rhodes. Credit: N. W. Ayer & Son, Inc.

The story of Kimberley is in part the story of Rhodes. Born in Hertfordshire, England, in 1853, the son of a rural clergyman, he was one of a dozen children. He was sickly as a child, suffering from tuberculosis. In 1870, at the age of seventeen, he left home to go to Natal, South Africa, where one of his brothers was a planter, hoping the climate might help him. Meanwhile the brother, Herbert, left to prospect for diamonds, found some and instructed Cecil to sell the plantation and join him at the diamond diggings. Cecil found diamonds elusive. He had to resort to selling drinking water to the miners to survive.

Out in the diamond fields, many of the mines were filling with water. Cecil saw an opportunity. He persuaded two Englishmen to join him in buying a pump at Port Elizabeth for £1,000. They rented it out to drain flooded claims. Soon they made enough money to buy more and better pumps from England.

Rhodes invested his profits in claims abandoned by disappointed miners or sold for pittances. Among the claims he succeeded in buying was a group owned by the brothers DeBeer, Joannes Nicholas, and Diedrich Arnoldus. By this time, however, Rhodes' tuberculosis flared up again. Unable to work hard, he returned to England to complete his education. He enrolled at Oxford and studied law.

Two years later, in 1873, with his health improved, he returned to South Africa. The claims he had left with his associates were producing diamonds. Now he used all his income to acquire more holdings. Rhodes saw that the day of the small prospector, working his claim with buckets, pick, and shovels was ending. He could visualize a vast diamond-mining industry requiring consolidation of properties and huge capital investments. Utilizing his legal training and his great persuasive powers, he engineered consolidations and mergers, increasing his own holdings with each move.

The story of Kimberley also is the story of Barney Barnato, London-born grandson of a rabbi. Barnato was only eighteen years old when he arrived on the scene in the same year that Rhodes returned to South Africa.

The two men were opposites. Rhodes had unreliable health, was tall and fair-skinned, scholarly in manner. Barnato was short, dark, and unruly, inclined to be noisy and unmannerly. They were to clash often.

Barney's real name was Barnett Isaacs. At fourteen he left school to follow his brother Harry to South Africa. His resources consisted of £100 and a watch given him as a parting present by friends.

Barney was bright enough to realize he would need all the capital he could get. Rather than spend his money on transportation, he walked alongside a wagon train for two months to make the trip from Cape Town to Kimberley. Rhodes sold water to make his start. Barney had invested in cheap cigars, which he traded to luxury-starved miners

*Barney **Barnato**. Credit: N. W. Ayer & Son, Inc.*

for small diamonds. These he used to buy more cigars which he traded for bigger and better diamonds. Early in his career he adopted the name of Barney Barnato in hopes of changing his luck, and Barnett Isaacs disappeared forever.

Barney learned all he could about diamonds from geologists. At that time, yellow earth on the surface was believed to be the chief source of diamonds. When miners dug through the yellow earth and reached a blue formation underneath, they went on to other fields. But geologists told Barney the yellow earth was simply a weathered form of the blue ground, and there was reason to believe additional riches would be found in the blue formations down deep. Barney gambled that the geologists were right. He bought up claim after claim on supposedly exhausted land in what is now known as the Kimberley pipe.

His ambition was to win control of the entire Kimberley pipe, some 1500 feet in diameter. In 1881, his opportunity arrived. A miner named Stewart, who owned several claims in the very center of the pipe, decided to sell his holdings. Bidding against several others, Barnato bought the claims for what was at that time considered a huge sum, £175,000. Many of Barnato's associates told him he had made a terrible mistake and that he could never recover his investment. Barnato was unimpressed.

About this time, Rhodes was distressed to see some of the property-owners embroiled in a bitter price war that finally led to diamonds being sold for less than the cost of production. He saw that the solution was controlled production at the source. Only a monopoly could prevent the ruinous competition. He decided to risk everything to acquire full control of all he could get his hands on. In order to do this, however, he had to control the Kimberley mine, which now belonged principally to Barnato.

Barney Barnato also realized a price war could jeopardize everything he owned. Barnato would have been satisfied to take control of the Kimberley mine and work out a plan of distribution with Rhodes. But Rhodes wanted undisputed control of South Africa's entire diamond industry, and, to accomplish this, the Kimberley field had to be brought into his organization. Thus began a gigantic battle for total control of the Kimberley.

The one large Kimberley mining firm which Barnato had not been able to acquire was a French enterprise, Compagnie Française de Diamant. Rhodes began quiet negotiations for this pivotal property. Given assurances that the company's entire stock could be had for £1,400,000, he hurried to London and persuaded the great banking house of Rothschild to lend him £1,000,000 to close the deal.

Barnato somehow learned of the proposed deal and

countered with an offer of £1,750,000 to the French company. At this point, Compagnie Française abruptly halted all negotiations with Rhodes.

Rhodes was stunned but wouldn't admit defeat. He made a personal visit to Barnato—the first time these men had met. Rhodes warned he was determined to acquire Kimberley's control at any cost. Then he offered Barnato a deal. Rhodes was to be allowed to pay the French company the original offer of £1,400,000. Then Rhodes would turn right around and sell the company to Barnato, at the same time paying £300,000 for a one-fifth interest in Barnato's company. It appeared to be a fine proposition. Barnato would get Compagnie Française's interest, which would consolidate his hold on the Kimberley. Rhodes' one-fifth interest couldn't interfere at all with Barnato's control of Kimberley Central Mining, but it would insure Barnato's cooperation in Rhodes' efforts to consolidate marketing efforts.

Barney Barnato agreed to the deal. The ink on the contract was no sooner dry than Rhodes made his move—and Barney discovered that he had greatly underestimated the almost maniacal ambitions of his rival.

Rhodes began offering unrealistically high prices for shares of Kimberley Central on the open market. Not even Barnato's friends could resist such offers, and they sold their shares to their friend's now bitter enemy.

While the battle for control was at its height, the price of diamonds was plunging, and both men realized they were engaged in a losing battle. Barnato was forced to capitulate. Rhodes dictated the terms: A new company would be formed, the DeBeers Consolidated Mines, Ltd., merging their interests. Barnato was given a huge block of stock and made a lifetime governor of the new company. However, his governorship was without power. The terms of the agreement prevented his interfering in any way with Rhodes' control of the company. The two men eventually became friends, and Barnato, with Rhodes' help, went on to become a member of the Cape Parliament. Rhodes also helped Barnato realize his ambition to become a member of the exclusive Kimberley Club.

But apparently these must have been superficial accomplishments in comparison to his ambitions, for Barney's colorful career came to an untimely end in 1897 when, at the age of forty-five, he apparently jumped overboard while on a voyage to England.

Rhodes, after consolidating his grip on the diamond industry, obtained a royal charter for the British South Africa Company. It was amazing in its scope. It gave him, among other things, the power to raise an army if necessary to insure proper protection and allowed him to expand the borders of Cape Colony as far as his capabilities permitted.

Minority stockholders of Kimberley Central were shocked at the terms of this most unusual charter and brought suit protesting the merger. The court agreed to a compromise whereby the Kimberley Central was allowed to liquidate its assets, and the new firm, DeBeers Consolidated, was permitted to purchase them. DeBeers issued a check for £5,338,650, a staggering sum at the time, and the canceled check is still a prized memento of the DeBeers Company. The pound was worth $5 then, but the investment was to repay itself many times over.

Now Rhodes was free to proceed with his plans. He developed gold mining, extended the railroad system, founded Rhodesia, and took part in the events which ultimately led to the Boer War between British and Dutch colonists.

He died in 1902, at a comparatively early age, as had Barnato. Rhodes was forty-nine.

His will granted a substantial fortune to Oxford University to found the now famous Rhodes Scholarships. They represent one of Rhodes' supreme purposes in life—to build a closer tie among English-speaking peoples. He was, foremost, an empire builder, and his chief beneficiary was the British Empire. He didn't care whose toes were stepped on in order to achieve his goals.

Rhodes' successors at DeBeers Consolidated Mines, Ltd., have carried out and even strengthened his policy of controlled supply. The world production of diamonds has become much larger and more complex than Rhodes ever dreamed possible, and the powerful DeBeers group has been able to assimilate new companies or persuade them to allow DeBeers to market their diamonds. This has meant dealing with a variety of governments and commercial interests. In most instances, DeBeers' executives have been able to demonstrate that diamond production and marketing can be regulated more satisfactorily for all through their central control.

In 1929, Sir Ernest Oppenheimer took over as chairman of DeBeers. When the world depression of the early 1930s threatened the very existence of the diamond industry, it was Sir Ernest who guided it to a firm financial footing. His son, Harry Oppenheimer, became head of DeBeers and he, too, acquired an admirable record by perpetuating the policies outlined by Rhodes and guiding the company through many problems which Rhodes never could have anticipated.

The diamond industry has had a fabulous growth. An old geography book which I acquired in my New York grammar school, published in 1905, has this interesting note.

> At Kimberley in Cape Colony are diamond mines, which now supply ninety-eight percent of all diamonds. The diamonds occur as crystals in a decomposed volcanic rock [they showed an illustration of Kimberley mine] and are obtained by carefully removing the crystals. After this the crystals must be cut into the proper shape and polished. There are various grades, some clear and beautiful, others impure and dull. So productive is this deposit of precious stones that $100,000,000 worth have been removed in eleven years. [Currently the output is approximately $500,000,000 per annum.] There is only a limited demand for diamonds; but the company in control is careful not to mine enough of them to reduce the price greatly. This is possible because the Kimberley mine owners have a practical monopoly of the diamond production of the world.

Monopolies are frowned on in America, but in a commodity which is pure luxury, like gem diamonds, wide and frequent price fluctuations could be disastrous. I believe that, were it not for the strong hand of DeBeers, the diamond world—a business involving billions of dollars—would be in constant jeopardy.

Kimberley, the legendary Diamond City, is still very much in the diamond business. Its four working mines produce more than 3,500,000 carats of gem and industrial quality stones annually. The citizens of Kimberley celebrated their centennial in 1971. Out of the blue ground of their great mine was laid the foundation of a great nation—and a great industry.

9

Mining: The Search for Needles in a Haystack

A most excellent diamond from the old rock.
—Anon.

There is no mining operation more complex than the recovery of diamonds; yet in some cases it is the simplest.

In 800 B.C., diamonds were literally picked up from the ground in India as they are today in some African countries. The first authentic reports to the Western world about diamonds and diamond recovery were made by Jean Baptiste Tavernier in the seventeenth century. He said as many as 50,000 men, women, and children worked in India's diamond fields. He described how they slaved under the hot sun in pits, carrying gravel to creeks for washing and picking out the diamonds by hand. Most mines were open pits, but he saw some tunnels bored into concentrations of ore. Spurred on by overseers armed with whips and watched by ever-present guards, the people systematically worked the first known source of diamonds in India in this manner.

The diamonds were so plentiful that even these primitive methods produced large quantities of the gems, including some like the Kohinoor, the Hope, and the Orloff. It is surprising that kimberlite pipes, the only known earth source of diamonds, were not found in India until recently.

In Brazil, where diamonds were found next, the miners used primitive techniques not unlike the gold recovery methods used by our own '49ers. Shallow pans filled with water were employed to wash the gravel with a rotary motion used to carry the lighter material away. Any diamonds left in the pan were extracted by hand. Later, sluiceboxes were operated by thousands of slaves, white and black.

Although their mines are substantially played out, the Brazilians are now using modern recovery methods in their search for new sources. In 1966, a 2400-ton bucket-line dredge was used with success. Brazil's diamonds are alluvial, and as yet no kimberlite pipes have been found.

South Africa was the next source, and, as we have found, mining methods were very crude at first. By 1872, 50,000 diggers had established themselves around Kimberley. Cecil Rhodes in a letter to his mother wrote: "Imagine a small round hill, at its highest only 30 feet above the level of the surrounding country, about 180-by-220 yards; a mass of white tents. It is like a great number of ant heaps covered with ants as thick as can be, the latter represented by human beings." The standard claim was only thirty feet square, but many of these were divided and subdivided.

At the start, the diggers pulverized the diamond-bearing ground with clubs and shovels, sifted the material in rocking troughs, and then sorted the dry gravel by hand. Pieces too large or too hard to be crushed were often just thrown away. In 1874, a big step forward was taken when water became available for rotary washing pans.

The miners thought at first that the diamonds all lay in shallow ground. But when it was learned that many were deep in the soil, the miners changed their tactics. As the men dug deeper and deeper, roads caved in, mine walls collapsed, and fights abounded over claim rights. Soon they struck water and shafts became flooded. Ropes and pulleys were used to haul soil to the surface. As the diggings got deeper, the danger of being buried alive or being injured by falling walls increased. Yet the lure of riches led the men on. After discovery of the first pipe mine, the Jagersfontein in 1870, and the Kimberley pipe the following year, more advanced techniques became necessary.

Deep down in the Premier mine, a crew prepares to blast out a section of diamond-bearing "blue ground." Credit: N. W. Ayer & Son, Inc.

Underground in a Kimberley mine, a conveyor belt carries broken "blue ground." Diamonds are deeply imbedded in these pieces. Credit: N. W. Ayer & Son, Inc.

This crusher recovers diamonds from the "blue ground." Credit: N. W. Ayer & Son, Inc.

A vertical shaft is sunk into the ground parallel to each of the pipes. Depending on the geology, the shafts might be as much as 1000 feet from the pipe. At intervals along the shaft, usually at levels of forty feet, horizontal tunnels are drilled into the kimberlite, which is then blasted loose and trundled out in mine cars. Elevators whisk the ore to treatment plants on the surface. There the blue ground (kimberlite) is screened for size. The larger chunks are carried by belts to crushers to be broken into smaller pieces. Then the crushed kimberlite is mixed with water in huge washers and stirred by metal rakes.

The diamond-bearing ore is then put into huge tanks of special liquid slightly lighter than the diamond's specific gravity of 3.52 so that the lighter waste materials are floated off while the heavier minerals, which would include the diamonds, sink to the bottom. The concentrate is then taken to grease tables, a remarkable invention.

Around 1897, a DeBeers engineer named Kirsten learned accidentally that the diamonds from pipe mines

Rough diamonds on a grease belt at a central treating plant. Credit: DeBeers Consolidated Diamond Mine, Ltd.

had a strange way of sticking to grease. When the concentrate was washed down a sloping table covered with grease, the diamonds stuck tenaciously to the grease while everything else was flushed away. Periodically the grease is scraped off the tables and heated. The diamonds are released when the grease melts, the gems are collected, cleaned, and made ready for marketing.

Though the same basic process continues to be used in some areas, improved ways are continually sought. One system is block caving. Through a series of operations, the kimberlite is made to break under its own weight. Safer for the miners and faster than former methods, it has proven quite successful.

Altogether different procedures are employed at the Consolidated Diamond Mines of South West Africa, where diamond-bearing gravels are buried under vast sand dunes.

First, prospect holes must be drilled to bedrock to

Sorting the diamonds is the final step in the recovery of these precious gems. Only twenty percent are suitable for cutting and polishing. Credit: N. W. Ayer & Son, Inc.

ascertain the depth of the sand overburden and the thickness of the diamond-bearing gravel bed. Once it has been determined that an area holds promise, the next step is removing the overburden. Often there are millions of tons of sand to be moved before the gravel is uncovered. Beneath the gravel is the bedrock, where potholes often hold a valuable cache of gemstones. These potholes are cleaned out by a machine like a giant vacuum cleaner, but the final step is sweeping out every crevice manually. However, this method is gradually fading out, in favor of hand work.

Consolidated Diamond Mines undoubtedly is the greatest continuous earth moving operation extant anywhere. In an average year, 25,000,000 tons of wind-blown sands are cleared for the recovery of 1,125,000 carats of diamonds, which means that twenty tons of sand are processed to find a single carat of diamonds. However, these are excellent gem diamonds, which makes this DeBeers'

This machine, the "vacuveyor," is a gigantic vacuum cleaner which sucks up possible diamond-bearing material from the bedrock. This method is gradually being phased out, as picking the diamonds by hand is growing more effective. One hundred million parts of sand and gravel must be removed to recover one part of diamonds. Credit: N. W. Ayer & Son, Inc.

currently most important and richest operation. One of the major problems is the storms that whip up huge waves which batter the beaches. The waves are held at bay by ingenious temporary sea walls while men and machines hurriedly delve down to bedrock to recover diamonds that otherwise might be buried forever by new mountains of sand.

Recovering diamonds from the sea itself is still another dramatic tale. The first efforts, as we have related, were made by the Barge 77 of Keeble and Collins. Anchored in 100 feet of water, a compressed hose was used to agitate the gravels at the bottom of the sea. They were then sucked up in a twelve-inch pipe and fed into a variety of washing jigs on the barge.

Now a prospecting vessel equipped with undersea drills is used to locate promising areas. When these have

Mining an open-cast diamond mine in Mirnyy, Russia. Credit: His Excellency Mr. Arnold Smith

been plotted out, a large barge recovery is towed to the designated locations. It employs methods considerably advanced over those developed in the pioneer Barge 77.

On the other hand, land operations create strange, difficult, and far different problems—especially in Siberia, with its 120-degree temperature range. The eight-month winters get to 70 degrees below zero, which means that the permafrost, which is hundreds of feet deep, must be warmed before it can be dug. Recovery plants need great quantities of running water, and somehow Soviet engineers have learned to overcome the problem. Their ability to make their machinery work under almost unbelievably frigid temperatures is, in itself, amazing.

One diamond mine north of the Arctic Circle is reported to have all buildings connected by heated tunnels, enabling the entire population to live and work all winter without leaving shelter.

In 1958, Russian technologists introduced an X-ray separation technique for diamonds at their mines in Yakutia in Siberia. A stream of gravel passes under an X-ray beam. Diamonds in the gravel light up when they

A view of a Siberian diamond mine, showing workers digging in the frozen ground. Credit: His Excellency Mr. Arnold Smith

pass the beam. The light impulse is picked up by a special tube which is coupled to an air-operated ejector. This, in turn, blows the diamonds out of the stream into a separate bin. A similar type of device has been developed at the DeBeers Research Laboratory in Johannesburg, based on the principle of X-ray luminescence. This separates dark and industrial diamonds from the concentrate. In time these machines may supplant the grease tables.

A view of the compound of a South African diamond mine. Credit: DeBeers Consolidated Diamond Mine, Ltd.

The mining of diamonds is now vastly complicated and costly, and each technological advance helps to make as full a recovery as possible. The work calls for skilled, dedicated labor. The standard of living is comparatively high for miners employed by such firms as DeBeers. Living quarters are comfortable and clean. Recreational facilities abound, and the workers are encouraged to partake in sports. Churches, free medical care, schools for children, and plenty of good food are the order of things. Training classes for workers who wish for different, more skilled types of work are available.

All in all, the industry has come a long way from the conditions described by Tavernier.

Diamonds in the rough are transformed into brilliant gems in the process of cutting. Rough diamonds may take a variety of shapes, as shown here. Whatever the shape, precise cutting is required to produce a diamond of maximum refraction and diffusion of light. Credit: N. W. Ayer & Son, Inc.

10

The Diamond Cutters

God's diamonds often cut one another.
—Thomas Fuller, *The Holy State*

Diamonds in the rough are seldom attractive. Only after they have been cut and polished to modern proportions do they acquire their dazzling beauty. It is amazing that they were prized and sought after in olden times.

In India, where diamonds were first found, the only way of improving their appearance was by rubbing one against another to achieve a sort of polish. In the thirteenth century, Venetian and French lapidaries experimented with faceting diamonds, and by the middle of the fifteenth century there was some real knowledge, thanks largely to a brilliant artisan of Bruges named Lodewyk van Berken, but better known as Louis de Berquem.

By this time, it had been learned that diamond dust, when impregnated with olive oil and smeared on a rapidly revolving disc, would polish diamonds. Today, 500 years later, the dust and oil are standard equipment in every diamond-cutting shop.

While some historians credit de Berquem with inventing the method, others put it a century earlier. Regardless, de Berquem used it to the fullest. He went to Paris to study mathematics, vital in diamond proportioning. Applying the knowledge gained from his studies, he improved faceting and proportioning to a remarkable degree, and he became the foremost diamond artisan of his time. As word of his skills spread, he was commissioned to fashion large diamonds for royalty of many nations. The great artists of his time, including Benvenuto Cellini, admired him

A statue of Louis de Berquem now standing in Antwerp, Belgium. Artist: Joe Barros. Credit: International Diamond Annual and Mr. A. N. Wilson

greatly. He gathered skilled workmen around him and he helped Antwerp develop a great diamond cutting industry. In the center of Antwerp stands a statue of the master wearing the jerkin and holster of his trade and with a diamond in his hand.

For the next century, constant efforts were made to find a cut which would release more of the diamond's fire and brilliancy. By the time of Cardinal Mazarin, the prime minister of Louis XIV, the round single-cut diamond came into being. It has 8 facets above the girdle (outside edge), 8 below, and the table (top octagonal facet). The cardinal was a lover and collector of diamonds, and it was said that he spent much of his spare time with diamond equipment. He popularized the single-cut diamond and is reputed to have invented it.

In the seventeenth century, a Venetian lapidary, Vincenti Peruzzi, invented the design which was the direct ancestor of the modern cut—the fifty-eight-facet "brilliant": thirty-two above the girdle, twenty-four below, the octagonal table, and the culet (extreme base). Each facet was ground with geometric precision, permitting the diamond for the first time to show its unique power of reflection, refraction, and dispersion. This all means that the brilliant-cut diamond takes in light, bends the rays, bounces them around within the stone, and then ejects them, broken down into the colors of the spectrum. Over the past 250 years, Peruzzi's model has been improved to further increase the attributes of his cut, but today's basic design is his, and no other shape since his time has been able to match the fire of a well-cut and proportioned brilliant-cut diamond.

Up to Peruzzi's time, and for years to follow, all diamond shaping had been done by grinding, which meant a tremendous waste of diamond material. It wasn't until the eighteenth century that the cutters found that a diamond could be sawed. This saved a great part of the diamond. Even with today's modern methods, up to half of a brilliant-cut diamond is lost; in Peruzzi's and de Berquem's days, the loss must have been tremendous.

In our own century—in 1919—a brilliant mathematician, Marcel Tolkowsky, devised a formula for angles and proportions for maximum fire and brilliancy which still is standard. Some minor changes have been made by some cutters, but his formula is considered the paragon by most cutters.

As practiced today, diamond cutting is a demanding and exacting art which allows for few errors. The gems are cut in one of two basic ways.

First, there is the brilliant, which includes the round and its variants: the pear shape, marquise, oval, and heart shape.

Second is the step cut, where the facets are in rows, such as the square cut or square emerald cut, the modified rectangular (better known as the emerald cut), and other

The characteristic diamond shape is an octahedron, roughly like two four-sided pyramids stuck together, base to base.

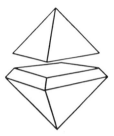

The rough stone is sawed into two parts.

Next it is "rounded" by grinding the corners away.

Then, when 58 facets have been polished on the rounded stone, the result is the standard brilliant cut.

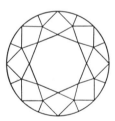

Top—33 facets   *Side view*   *Bottom—25 facets*

Diagram showing how a diamond is cut to produce maximum fire and brilliancy. Credit: Gemological Institute of America

shapes where the facets are in steps, or rows, above and below the girdle (outer edge).

As the great majority of diamonds are round, the standard round brilliant cut is most common.

Not long ago a new style called the "Barion" cut was announced by Basil Watermeyer, who worked for years trying to improve the brilliancy of step-cut diamonds (emerald cut, square cut, etc.). He is associated with Jooste's Cutting Works of Johannesburg, South Africa, patent holders of the Barion cut. This is a combination of the top of the square or emerald cut with a form of brilliant cut lower half which, it is Jooste's claim, gives the diamond more brilliancy. The Barion might well be an exciting improvement in diamond cutting.

Antwerp is the center of diamond cutting, with approximately 15,000 workmen. It has been the largest producer of finished gem diamonds for decades. Israel is very close behind. Its diamond-cutting facilities have grown tremendously in a comparatively short period, and it now threatens to overtake the leaders.

Amsterdam, which was a world leader before World War II, lost its position when the factories were demolished. Dutch cutters now number only 800 or 900, which is far below the prewar level of several thousands.

The United States has fine cutting plants, mostly in New York where some of the largest and finest stones are

Diamond cutting plant of Katz and Lebovics, Johannesburg. Credit: Peter Holz

cut. The United Kingdom, Republic of South Africa, the U.S.S.R., France, West Germany, and a comparative newcomer, Japan, all have modern diamond-cutting plants. Other major cutters are Portugal, Puerto Rico, and the Scandinavian countries.

India, where it all started, has thousands of cutters —perhaps more than any other country—but they work mostly as individuals or in small groups, so there are no available figures. The standard of their work has not been comparable to that of other countries, but it is constantly improving. In time, they will undoubtedly be an important factor in the cutting world.

An interesting development is the Winston diamond-cutting plant in Chandler, Arizona, where about 100 American Indians from several different tribes are doing excellent work.

The object of cutting is to transform the rough crystal into a sparkling gem. In the process, as many flaws as possible must be eliminated, with an ever-watchful eye to the retention of all possible weight.

At the top in any cutting shop is the planner, usually a skilled veteran who is familiar with all the intricacies of the art. It is his responsibility to determine whether as large a stone as possible should be cut from the rough—or whether it be more economical to obtain several smaller stones. He must decide whether it will be better to saw or cleave the stone, or both. He must also determine what shapes can best be obtained from the crystal.

The first step is the study of the crystal. On larger stones, "windows" may be polished on the surface so the interior can be examined.

Diamonds are usually sawed, but occasionally it is more advantageous to cleave them. Each diamond has a molecular structure that might be compared to the grain in a piece of wood. Diamonds may be cleaved only along the line of molecular "grain," so it is necessary to know how the grain runs in planning the ultimate shape of the gem. Usually this is no problem, but sometimes prolonged inspection and study are necessary, especially if the stone

When a diamond is divided with its grain, it is set in a dop and a groove is scratched with another diamond. A cleaving knife is set in the groove and tapped with a palm-wood hammer. If the stone has been properly marked and grooved, it will split cleanly. If not, it may shatter into bits. Credit: N. W. Ayer & Son, Inc.

has a shape difficult to define. In many cases, it is necessary to study a stone for days—and even months.

If cleaving is called for, the cleavage plane is determined and the place at which the stone is to be cleaved is decided. Then a tiny groove is made in the stone with a diamond-pointed tool. Progressively larger diamonds are used until the groove reaches the desired proportions. The blade of a steel wedge is then held in the groove and

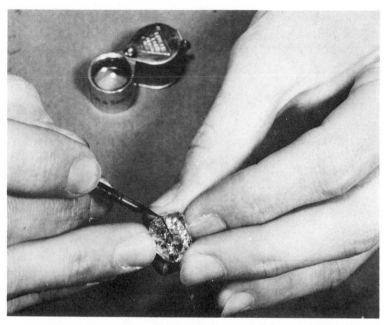

An expert examines a diamond through a powerful magnifying glass—the "loupe" shown above—to see how the stone can be cut for maximum weight. After studying the stone's imperfections, he marks the diamond where it must be divided. Credit: N. W. Ayer & Son, Inc.

struck with a light metal rod or wooden mallet. This is a critical operation and needs knowledge and a steady hand. Many diamonds have been shattered by an inexpertly directed blow.

We read of instances in olden days when Oriental potentates stood over their diamond cutters as they worked, ready to order them punished if they made a faulty move. Those were working conditions hardly conducive to steadying nerves!

Oddly enough, while cleaving is becoming a less frequently used technique, two of the most important cleaving jobs of all time, the Cullinan and the Jonker, have been done in this century.

In sawing, the diamond is cut against the grain. Each stone is marked for sawing in India ink by one of the head workmen and is mounted in a holder called a dop.

These diamonds have been marked with India ink for sawing. Each diamond has a grain, like that of wood, that is apparent to an expert. Credit: N. W. Ayer & Son, Inc.

In this picture, the three larger stones are cemented in dops and marked. The dop at the lower right holds one part of a sawed diamond; the other part is at the left.

The sawing is done by a circular disk about three inches in diameter. Impregnated with a mixture of diamond dust and olive oil (only diamond can cut diamond), the disk is as thin as a sheet of ordinary paper and revolves in a belt driven machine at about 4500 revolutions per minute.

After the diamond is divided, the next step is called girdling, bruting, or rounding, which means shaping the stone at its greatest width. This is done by mounting the diamond on a lathe which revolves at high speed. Another diamond, mounted on a long straight stick held under the operator's arm, is held against the rotating diamond. Each

When a diamond is cut, it is clamped into an arm above the saw so that the blade cuts along the marked line. The edge of a phosphor-bronze saw blade, only 35/10,000 inch thick, is coated with a paste of diamond dust and oil to create a cutting surface. The blade turns at a high speed. A small diamond may take hours to cut; a larger diamond may take days. Credit: N. W. Ayer & Son, Inc.

stone wears down and shapes the other. All diamond dust and chips are caught and saved for industrial purposes.

At this stage, there is still no sign of the diamond's ultimate luster. That comes in the final two steps.

The blocker now takes over and gives the diamond its principal facets. The work is done on a heavy cast iron wheel called a scaif. Carefully adjusted and balanced, it spins at about 3000 r.p.m. The blocker gives the stone eight facets and the table (the octagonal plane at the top of each round diamond) on top, and eight facets below the girdle. Small diamonds are cut with only these seventeen facets and are called single cut, as opposed to the full cut which has fifty-eight facets.

The final step is that of the brillianteerer.

After a diamond has been divided, each part is finished as a separate gem. The next step is "girdling" or "bruting," shaping the diamond at its greatest width. For the round or "brilliant" cut, the stone is mounted on a lathe that revolves at high speed, rounding the gem with another diamond that is held on a long stick. Credit: N. W. Ayer & Son, Inc.

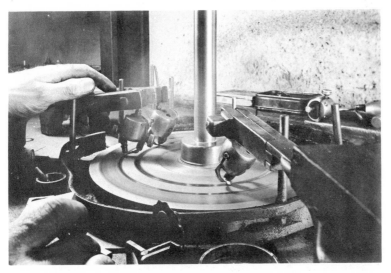

The final step in cutting is placing the diamond's facets or planes. Most diamonds have fifty-eight facets—thirty-three above the girdle, twenty-five below. For this operation, the stone is set in a holder against a revolving iron disk that has been impregnated with oil and diamond dust. Credit: N. W. Ayer & Son, Inc.

He grinds the remaining facets until all fifty-eight are shaped—thirty-two facets above the girdle, twenty-four below, the table, and culet. Occasionally the culet (the very bottom facet) is eliminated, but usually a very tiny, almost imperceptible one is left. It is a precaution against chipping. The brillianteerer will correct minor errors made in blocking, and he polishes away wheel marks. So skilled is he that he can judge the all-important facet angles by the eye alone.

Thus the diamond, under the trained eyes of the workers, emerges as the most beautiful gemstone extant. Frequently all the operations are done by a single cutter.

Because it takes so long to saw even a very small diamond, a modern plant has many saws going at one time. Once the diamond is set on the saw blade, the procedure is automatic, but the skilled operator must check each saw frequently to make sure that the cut is going properly. In many shops, semi-automatic machines take over other aspects of diamond cutting.

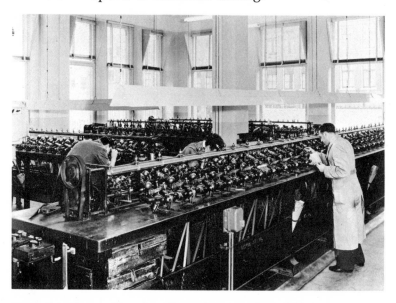

Rows of cutting machines in a diamond-cutting plant. Skilled sawyers check frequently to make sure the cut is going properly and that the blade is coated with diamond paste. Credit: N. W. Ayer & Son, Inc.

A selection of finished diamonds at Goldmuntz Polishing Works, Antwerp.
Credit: Goldmuntz Polishing Works

Countless fine stones have been ruined by inept cutters. One of the most notable is the Great Mogul diamond,
which was entrusted to a Venetian cutter named Hortensio Borgio in the seventeenth century. This great diamond
weighed 787.5 carats when found in India. Borgio's inept-
ness reduced it to 280 carats. The Mogul Aurangzeb was
so furicus that he refused to pay for the work and fined
the cutter his entire fortune, which, of course, didn't make
up for the loss. In an earlier era, poor Borgio might have
lost his head.

11

From Mine to Milady

We shall see the whole sky all diamonds.
—Chekhov in *Uncle Vanya*

MARKETING AND DISTRIBUTION

Once the diamonds leave the mines, they pass through many hands in a complex process before reaching your jeweler. In the first step, they are sorted, gem from industrial, for size and color. Most then are sent to London, the world headquarters for the diamond industry. A smaller percentage goes to Kimberley.

In the London offices of the Diamond Trading Company, an arm of the DeBeers organization, the gemstones are separated into individual parcels to be shown to a small group of buyers from all over the world. This group, made up of cutters, large dealers, and wholesalers, numbers only about 200.

To become a member of this select body, a person must be well-established in his field, have an unimpeachable reputation and adequate financial resources, and be an aggressive businessman. Thousands of dealers with these attributes would love to be regular customers of the Diamond Trading Company, but the firm takes the attitude that its small nucleus of carefully chosen buyers can do the job better.

Serving as intermediaries between the buyers and the Diamond Trading Company are the brokers. There are fewer than a dozen of them. They perform one of the most unusual and specialized functions to be found anywhere in any field. It is they, either an individual or a firm, who

Diamond sorters separating gemstones into parcels that will be shown to buyers from all over the world. Credit: N. W. Ayer & Son, Inc.

deal with the customers. The broker must know his customers and their problems. He must have an understanding of world conditions as a whole and the economic conditions of the client's country as well or better than the client himself. He must be as nearly infallible as possible in the advice he offers. He must be able to speak the language of his client as well as English to maintain the closest of relationships.

The broker travels to his client's country several times a year to learn his needs, to advise the customer about the goods which should be asked for, and about the size and qualities of his probable allotments. The broker must know better than the buyer what types of goods are selling best. The broker may plead on behalf of his client for more goods, more variety, or other needs from the Diamond Trading Company. If the Company is not able to grant the request, the broker must relay the refusal to the buyer with diplomatic skill.

Finally, if the client is unable to attend a "sight"—a showing of stones—the broker might have to do his buying for him. The broker is a highly specialized jack-of-all-trades in diamond business; but also he must be master of all.

The brokers are an institution, and without them an intricate business would become far more so. The Company, through the brokers, gets a good idea of the type of diamonds the customer has most need of and does its best to fill those needs satisfactorily. With the broker's guidance, the Company makes up the parcels for the buyer's inspection. Traditionally they are called sights.

There are ten sights each year in London, and invitations to attend them are mailed to the chosen buyers with a query as to size and qualities preferred.

I had always wanted to be present at a sight, and it was my good fortune to be invited to observe one. In the main room are tables with northern exposure—diamonds are best judged for color by north light. (In Johannesburg or Kimberley, in the Southern Hemisphere, the exposure for sights is southern.) Away from the main room are small rooms for the clients. Here the diamonds may be examined at leisure. Each man has his own magnifier, or loupe, for close-up inspection of individual stones.

Cardboard boxes are brought in. In them are stones wrapped in folded papers. Each buyer pays the same price for stones of equal size and quality, although the size of the purchase may vary from customer to customer. The invoices accompanying the stones may total millions of dollars.

At this point, the procedure differs from all other diamond buying. The customer is not permitted to say which papers he would like to buy and which he would like to reject. The lot was made up for him especially, with the advice and help of his broker, and he must buy it all or none. And there is no haggling about price.

His box may contain more small stones than he would

Buyers examine diamonds at a "sight" in the Diamond Trading Company's office in London. Credit: DeBeers Consolidated Diamond Mines, Ltd.

like (there are never too many large ones) or some with color he might like exchanged. But it is his box and he must take it or leave it in its entirety. All transactions are for cash.

It is understood that, if an allotment is refused, the buyer may not get another invitation to attend a sight for some time. However, if the buyer has a valid reason for

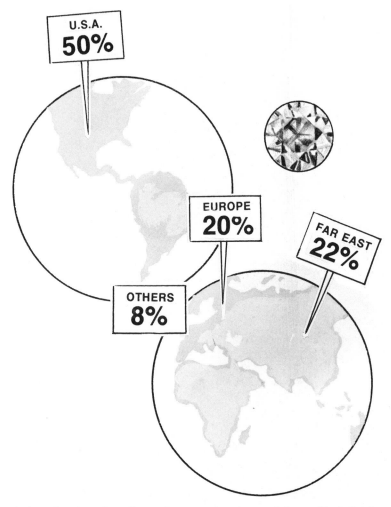

A chart showing where diamonds are purchased around the world. Artist: Joe Barros

refusing his lot—a major economic depression in his country, for example—the Company is reasonable.

From the Company's point of view, it must sell the poor as well as the good diamonds or else it is in trouble. All the buyers would prefer the better qualities if they had a choice, but the Company plays no favorites and allots some of each quality to all its clientele.

In the business of mining diamonds, the Company

couldn't afford to be left with the poorer stones while selling only the premium qualities. Through this system, each purchaser is able to buy the goods at advantageous prices. Each is free to resell the stones he doesn't want to members of the various diamond "clubs," so he is not hurt by the method.

The Company makes it a policy of remaining in a very liquid position. Thus, when a break in economic conditions takes place, as happened in 1969 and 1970, DeBeers has the resources to keep mining machinery rolling at full blast, which must be the case in this type of business. They have the means to stockpile when necessary and to reduce dealer allotments in poor times. In any case, the system has proven satisfactory through the years, and I have never heard of a disgruntled client giving up his privilege of buying at a sight.

There are four diamond bourses in Antwerp, all on crowded Pelikaanstraat. Credit: John Brett Cohen, Optima *Magazine*

A diamond bourse in Antwerp. Credit: John Brett Cohen, Optima *Magazine*

The over eighty percent of the world supply controlled by DeBeers is sold in this manner. From the sights, the stones are sent to the headquarters of the buyers or to cutters in Antwerp, Israel, the United States, Holland, the United Kingdom, and other cutting centers. Eventually, in cut form in most cases, the stones will be sent to the diamond clubs, where they are sold to the wholesale and retail jewelers of their countries. New York, with two such clubs, handles the greatest percentage of diamonds in America.

The diamond clubs, too, are very selective about members. There are only about two dozen clubs in the world, and total membership doesn't exceed 10,000. Each applicant must have a spotless record and must be highly recommended by several members before he can qualify.

Unlike the quiet dignity of the London sights, where it all starts, the world's diamond clubs are beehives of activity. My wife and I spent many exciting hours in the Antwerp club watching the dealers buying and selling a profusion of diamonds at a frantic pace.

Israel, which has shown incredible growth in very few years, recently has erected a twenty-eight-story building

The Israel Diamond Building in Ramat Gan. Largest in the world devoted to diamonds. Credit: Yehuda Appelberg

A corner of the Israel Diamond Bourse. Credit: Starphoto Agency, Tel Aviv

in Ramat Gan to house its diamond activities. It is the largest single building in the world devoted entirely to diamond merchandising. It houses more than 250 firms from over a score of countries. Included are three banks, offices of the Diamond Controller and Customs Department, the post office, the Bourse's large trading hall, and the great vaults where rough and polished goods are kept. A thousand people occupy the offices; each day more than $1,000,000 in raw and finished gems are traded. Israel's diamond center is an amazing sight, indeed.

My first visit to one of New York's diamond clubs was an unforgettable experience. As a guest, I was whisked up an elevator, passed through a phalanx of plainclothesmen, identified, and taken through thick bulletproof, electrically operated doors to get to the main trading room. Men of all ages, some bearded, some clean-shaven, of every description and nationality, were bargaining in every known language—and, it seemed to me, some unknown languages. There were calls for individuals on the public address system. Messengers flitted to and fro. Voices rose as buyers haggled over prices. Everyone seemed to know everyone else.

Despite the seeming confusion, business is done on a very exemplary basis. Mutual trust prevails and the word of each member is as good as his bond. Once a price is agreed upon and a deal is made, the principals shake hands and the seller wishes the buyer *"Mazel und broche,"* the ancient traditional term meaning good luck and blessings. Jews and non-Jews alike use the expression. No deal in any club is official until *"Mazel und broche"* has been uttered. That, with a hand clasp, binds the deal, from which there is no backing out.

If a dispute should arise, an infrequent occurrence, there is a Board of Arbitrators in the club to settle the matter. If the disputants don't abide by the findings of the Board, as stated in the by-laws, one or both may be disbarred. If this should occur, notices are sent to the World Federation in Antwerp, which notifies all the diamond clubs of the world. This is tantamount to an automatic end to the individual's connection with the wholesale diamond business.

Forbes Magazine summed it up very well in an article on the diamond business: "A strange business, diamonds. On the one end, modern merchandising and promotion; on the other end DeBeers, a global monopoly. And in between an anachronistic, almost Old Testament world, older than capitalism and yet perfectly fitted to it."

The final link in the diamond distribution chain is the retail jeweler. In the United States, 25,000 retail jewelery stores sell diamonds and jewelry running into the billions of dollars. It is big business even by American standards and a far cry from the tiny start made in New York City's Maiden Lane when the first jewelry and silversmithing shops made their appearance in the late 1700s.

Some of the retail stores are family-owned businesses; others are part of large chains. While the small merchant sells an occasional diamond from his limited stock, the larger jeweler may make many and more impressive sales because he can offer better selections. Knowledge of diamonds is often on a higher plane in the larger stores. Higher remuneration helps to produce salesclerks who have the knowledge to answer questions about diamonds other than the size of the stone, its price, and payment procedures.

Leading jewelers today study diamonds and other gems by reading the many excellent trade magazines; with the aid of their trade associations they keep up with developments within the industry. No small part of this is due to the efforts of the prestigious Gemological Institute of America (G.I.A.). A nonprofit organization dedicated to assist the jewelry industry, it has wielded great influence since it was founded more than forty years ago.

Robert M. Shipley, who had studied gemology in England and France, saw the need for such an organization and formed the Institute in 1931. He devoted all his efforts to developing the Institute until his retirement in 1952. Subsequently, it has continued to grow in importance.

There aren't very many jewelers who have the knowledge and skills which are necessary to distinguish them as professionals. The assistance available to them through the facilities of the Institute has been a priceless asset.

The basic purpose of the G.I.A. is to train jewelers in gem identification, grading, and appraising through the use of modern instruments, many of which were developed in G.I.A.'s own laboratories. Resident classes and home study courses have been made available to thousands. In addition, G.I.A. sends instructors and equipment to various cities for the benefit of jewelers unable to attend the resident classes. Above all, the Institute stresses integrity and high ethics. It has headquarters in Los Angeles under the direction of Richard T. Liddicoat, who was personally trained by founder Shipley. The New York laboratory is under the direction of Robert Crowningshield, one of the world's foremost gemologists. Diplomas are awarded to those who have completed their various courses, and these are displayed with as much pride as those of any physician or attorney.

In the more than half century I have spent in the jewelry business, I have seen a vast upgrading in the level of knowledge about diamonds among store owners and salespersons. This is good for both the industry and the public. As more and more jewelers avail themselves of the facilities of the G.I.A., the needed knowledge and high ethics espoused will place the jeweler on a higher plane than ever in his chosen profession.

On another plane, the industry has sought to stimulate interest in the designing of jewelry through what is known as the Diamonds-International Awards. The event

The symbol of the Diamonds-International Awards. Credit: N. W. Ayer & Son, Inc.

Winning diamond pieces at vario
Diamonds-International Award
from 1965–1972.

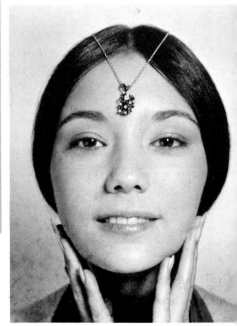

is sponsored by DeBeers Consolidated Mines, Ltd., under the auspices of N. W. Ayer and Son, Inc. Judges are selected internationally.

The first awards were made in 1954 to American jewelers. So much interest was shown that by 1957 the awards became worldwide in scope. That year, sixty-five designers were represented. By 1972, 1295 designers from thirty-five countries submitted entries.

The annual contest is primarily for professional jewelers, with awards going to some of the best-known names in the industry here and abroad; but anyone interested in jewelry design is eligible. Style trends are frequently indicated by the designs submitted each year.

Each year jewelry selected by members of the Diamonds-International Academy is shown at the famous Diamond Ball in New York. The Academy is made up of designers who have won at least three Diamonds-International Awards. The ball, which is for the benefit of the Institute of International Education, is one of the highlights of the social season.

The award, which is a wooden plaque with a metal bas-relief of a goddess of beauty, is as highly coveted as the Oscars presented by the Academy of Motion Picture Arts and Sciences. Marking excellence in each field, the award insures recognition of merit and ability.

The success of Diamonds-International Awards competition led in 1970 to an annual competition for American designers only. Called the American Diamond Jewelry Competition, its purpose is to encourage creative design and imaginative use of small diamonds in women's and men's jewelry.

To my surprise and pleasure, I was selected to be one of the three judges for the 1972 event at the St. Moritz Hotel in New York City. The other judges were Robert L. Green, fashion editor of *Playboy* magazine, and Vera, the famous designer.

I was impressed not only by the great variety of excellent and imaginative designs, but with the fairness with which the affair was handled. The entries were designated

The author, left, *with fellow judges for the 1972 American Diamond-Jewelry Competition in New York–Mrs. Vera Newmann, fashion designer, Vera, and Robert L. Green, fashion editor,* Playboy Magazine. *Credit: N. W. Ayer & Son, Inc.*

by number only; names of the entrants were known only to the sponsors. It was regrettable that we couldn't give awards to all of the excellent pieces of jewelry submitted.

12

The Seamy Side of Diamonds

O Diamond! Diamond! Thou little knowest the mischief done!
—Thomas Maude in the poem *Wensley-Dale*

Because diamonds are immensely valuable and easily hidden, they are the targets of thieves, smugglers, and their kindred fellows at every stage of production and distribution. The stakes are high and, as with narcotics, there is never a lack of traffickers. In fact, the illicit traffic in rough diamonds in some countries is reportedly equal to that of legitimate sources.

In the days when industrial diamonds were scarce, the Soviet Union had to rely on a huge flow of smuggled diamonds from Central Africa to manufacture precision instruments for its hydrogen bomb and intercontinental ballistic missiles programs. Without them, Soviet efforts would have been delayed for years.

Liberia in some years exports three times as many diamonds as it produces. Oddly enough, while much of Liberia's output is industrial quality, its exports are predominantly fine gem quality. One can suspect the gems are smuggled in from neighboring Sierra Leone, which has more theft problems with uncut diamonds than any country in Africa. Some of the thievery is quite open.

In November 1969, bandits threw pepper in the eyes of security men of Sierra Leone Selection Trust, Ltd., a British South African firm, and got away with $3,600,000 worth of its diamonds. *The New York Post* reported "poachers by the thousands" dig up diamonds from this firm's property and smuggle them to other countries—and little is done to stop it. The report went on to say diamond exports from Sierra Leone amounted to $60,000,000.

But Liberia, a southeastern neighbor where diamonds are found only on a comparatively small scale, has diamond exports of almost $40,000,000. Most of them were smuggled from Sierra Leone, officials say. And Liberia isn't the only place where diamonds smuggled from Sierra Leone wind up.

The poachers dig on Selection Trust's property in broad daylight, sometimes waving to company helicopters with security officers who can do little because they can't carry arms. There are also some poachers who fear no action against them because, they boast, they can buy anybody off. Selection Trust complains the government does little to protect its diamond fields. There have been crackdowns. Some foreign poachers and smugglers have been deported, but they come right back.

The output of Sierra Leone is entirely alluvial, the quality of the diamonds is exceptionally fine, and this compounds their problems. Selection Trust engages a large security force, but many are easily corrupted as the stakes are high, so investigators are sent in, and then investigations are made of the investigators.

Illicit diamond miners in Sierra Leone. Credit: Newsweek Photo by Andrew Jaffe (Copyright, Newsweek, 1972)

In February 1972, *Newsweek* reported that 60,000 free-lance miners in Sierra Leone work day and night gathering illicit gems. Guards posted at the Liberian border, the report said, pass luggage for a bribe as small as $10. The lengthy *Newsweek* article added that the government sent in the army several years ago to drive off the illicit diggers but soon had to pull the troops out. They were digging, too.

Despite the efforts of DeBeers, the International Diamond Security Organization, Interpol, and the special diamond detective departments of the police in such a trading center as Johannesburg, the problem of illicit diamond trading remains largely unsolved. It takes only a few dishonest persons at each step of the diamond industry to smuggle an enormous amount of gems into illegitimate channels.

Even in the pipe mines, where security is on a much sounder basis, thefts are relatively easy. A fluoroscope technician, after completing his search of a worker, might hand him a bag of diamonds to be carried out of the plant. For crossing borders, secret compartments of unbelievable ingenuity are made to hide the gems, for example, special pockets in a woman's brassiere.

Specially designed brassieres for hiding diamonds are not a new story. In the early 1930s, I was in a third-class coach of a train bound from Cairo to Port Saïd. It was during the Great Depression and third class was cheapest, but let's say I was also looking for local color. My seat was a wooden bench by an open window; there was no air-conditioning, although there were plenty of cinders. My seat was shared with a plump native woman who took up two-thirds of it. Shortly after we left the Cairo station, she started to unbutton her blouse and fumbled with her brassiere. My thoughts immediately flashed to stolen diamonds.

As I watched incredulously—after all, she was practically sitting on me—she removed a tiny cup from under an ample breast and from under the other a small metal container. She then proceeded to enjoy a coffee break, Arab style. Presumably the container was being kept warm under her blouse. Afterward, she dried the cup on her not-too-clean skirt. She replaced both cup and container and then sighed contentedly as she buttoned her blouse. No diamonds.

In the early days of pipe mining in South Africa, native workmen were kept virtually imprisoned for long periods to make sure they didn't walk off with concealed diamonds. After working hours, they were confined in walled enclosures with barred gates while armed guards watched over them. But even these measures didn't stop thievery. Sometimes stones were catapulted outside the compounds to waiting confederates. Occasionally a workman swallowed so many diamonds he was hospitalized because his pains gave him away. Swallowing stones just before a worker's term was up became so prevalent that it became the custom to detain men for physical examinations for several days following the termination of their contracts.

Conditions are vastly improved now in the DeBeers mines. Bonuses are paid to those who uncover large stones. Fluoroscopes and X-ray machines, while used sparingly, help to discourage temptation. But workers do try now and again. In Windhoek, South West Africa, two diamond mine workers were charged with attempting to steal ninety-two diamonds worth $20,000 by wrapping them in "X-ray–proof" lead in their hollowed shoe heels.

In a South American diamond-producing country it is widely known that government statistics don't reflect the real output. Only a portion is declared, the balance being sold secretly by mine owners to avoid payoff to officials. Similarly, it is a simple matter for dishonest officials to overlook diamonds carried on the persons of certain favored gentlemen when leaving the country for European cutting centers.

Fortunately, not even official position can protect smugglers from dedicated lawmen. Not long ago a high-ranking Peruvian judge was arrested at John F. Kennedy Airport in New York when a customs agent became curi-

Custom agents seized this wooden case which contained $200,000 in diamonds. Two sides of the wooden packing case had been hollowed out to conceal the diamonds. Credit: World Wide Photos

ous about a bulge in his trousers. It turned out to be a bag of diamonds. Another bulge, another bag. The agent then reached into the Peruvian's pockets, and three more bags of diamonds were found. The haul was valued at $100,000.

Newsweek told of a sixty-year-old Brazilian miner who discovered a dirt-encrusted diamond almost the size of a golf ball near the town of Portas dos Diamantes, not far from Brasilia, the capital. He had, fittingly enough, been issued mining license 007, and his story could have been the script of a James Bond story except that justice didn't triumph in the end.

Instead of turning the stone in to his employer, the miner took it to his shack and showed it to his wife and children. The wife tucked it away in her bosom for safekeeping until he could sell it. Meanwhile, he traced its shape on a page from the Bible, apparently to record its size. Some days later, after a few mellowing drinks in a

Another trick in the illicit diamond trade—a hollow clothes-brush that was seized by U.S. Customs Agents in New York. The brush contained a hundred carats of uncut diamonds, valued at $50,000. Credit: Wide World Photos

tavern, the miner felt he just had to confide his secret to the Greek owner of the bar. The Greek offered him a check for $1800—and the diamond changed hands. When the check proved worthless, the miner went to the police. By then the Greek was in Athens, the stone with him.

Two months later, he returned to Brazil. He had a story ready for the police. The alleged diamond, he asserted, was only a rock crystal. This he discovered when he accidentally dropped it and it split into several pieces. The police investigator took this story, understandably enough, with a grain of salt and decided to cut himself in on the deal. He kidnaped the Greek and tortured him to get the truth. Shortly thereafter, the police investigator, a fellow detective, and a Brazilian congressman flew to Athens disguised as Interpol agents and went to a certain garden where they believed the stone was buried. But the Greek police had been expecting them and all were jailed except the congressman, who claimed immunity. Meanwhile, the Greek bar owner was subjected to the tender mercies of a gang of roughnecks headed by the original finder of the diamond. The cops jailed both the miner and the Greek.

Case 007, as it was becoming known, was now a national *cause célèbre*. The chief of Brazil's federal police wrote an official report. This was challenged by the congressman, who countercharged that the chief of police was implicated in the affair. The chief, summoned by President Castelo Branco, resigned shortly after the meeting.

A congressional investigating committee was held with public hearings. The Greek insisted that the diamond was not real, although he was overheard telling cellmates that an accomplice was having the diamond cut and sold. No one seems to know what happened to the diamond. Experts who examined the drawing made in the Bible estimated that it must have weighed 400 carats, worth perhaps as much as $5,000,000.

Newspaper reports of large diamond robberies are almost routine, but sometimes a heist is executed with such flair that it becomes notable. "New York Gem Theft like Hitchcock Thriller," a headline screamed recently. Involved were $250,000 in gems, police armed with an electric eye that peers into the night, a gang of acrobatic thieves, and a mad scramble for the jewelry tossed out a window. A burglar alarm had brought police to the eighteenth floor of a twenty-story midtown Manhattan building. They scanned the darkness with the electronic device which magnifies available light more than 100 times, developed for night fighting in Viet Nam, and focused on a man hanging by a rope from the second floor window.

Out of the same window four other men were throwing cases of diamond rings taken from a vault smashed with sledgehammers. One of the cases broke, scattering rings all over the courtyard. The man dangling from the rope was arrested, but the others escaped.

Another sensational case was the raid on New York's posh Hotel Pierre early in 1972, when bandits looted the hotel strong box of hundreds of thousands of dollars in diamond jewelry. Two smartly dressed men carrying suitcases stepped out of an elegant limousine at 4 A.M. in front of the locked hotel entrance, summoned the lobby guard, and said they had reservations. When the guard opened the door, the men whipped out pistols and systematically ransacked the safety deposit boxes. An hour and a half later, they calmly sped away with their loot.

Switch artists who substitute glass for real stones are as old as time, but once in a while there is an unusual twist. A diamond setter once told me of a man who came to his place with a loose diamond and a mounting. "I want to sit right here and watch you do the setting," the man said. "I don't trust anyone."

The setter told me, "That made me so mad, that right under his very eyes, I substituted a poorer diamond for his." I suppose this might be called a mitigating circumstance.

Crooks come up with such ingenious schemes to defraud that we wonder why these people don't apply their brains to making an honest living. Consider the poor jeweler who told this sad tale. He received a call from a "Father Kelly," who said he was calling from the hospital room of a prominent woman known to the jeweler. He explained she and her boyfriend had decided to become engaged and wanted to see some diamond rings. However, they wanted to keep the engagement a secret, so "Father Kelly" agreed to act as go-between. The jeweler was instructed to meet "Father Kelly" with the diamonds at the emergency entrance because of parking problems. The jeweler brought two large diamond engagement rings which he left with the fully robed "priest." The good "father" suggested the jeweler have a cup of coffee while he took the diamonds to the patient. And that's the last the jeweler saw of either the rings or the "priest."

Inez Robb, the journalist, wrote a widely reprinted column titled *How King of Diamonds Was Trumped*. It was about a well-dressed woman who swindled two of New York's most prestigious jewelry establishments—Tiffany's and Harry Winston, Inc.—in a matter of five to seven minutes late one January afternoon in 1965. She was never found. Harry Winston, the "King of Diamonds," doubts that she ever will be because "the woman was an amateur and got all the breaks of her amateur status" in her desperate longing for a magnificent diamond ring. Winston told Miss Robb:

"First, she went into Tiffany's. There, in what is known as 'the great diamond switch robbery,' she coolly exchanged the 2.75-carat marquise diamond she was wearing for a 3.69-carat marquise diamond valued at $19,800.

"Now the ring she was wearing when she entered Tiffany's was a good diamond, worth $7500. If she had been a real thief, she would never have left behind a diamond valued at $7500 when she could have substituted a cheap one.

"It probably took her two minutes to walk from Tiffany's to my place. She was then wearing a $19,800 diamond. She had never been in my showroom before. When such a new customer arrives, an employee who knows our clientele pushes a little button and a red light glows in an inner office. Though she looked like a lady, was dressed like a lady, and behaved like one, she was never out of surveillance of two employees, one a former F.B.I. man."

She calmly switched Tiffany's 3.69 marquise diamond ring valued at $19,800 for a Winston marquise valued at $38,500 and weighing 5.30 carats. Then she walked out and vanished.

"She was an amateur, you can be sure," Winston told Miss Robb. "No real gem thief would have left that fine Tiffany diamond in exchange for my larger one. She just wanted a beautiful diamond. And she has one. Mine."

And while Winston takes the whole diamond-substitute caper philosophically, "he does not go so far as to wish that the woman wear his ring in good health."

What becomes of stolen jewelry? Amateurs in their hurry to dispose of the loot are often caught. The professionals who know the ropes get it to fences, without whom the number of jewelry and other robberies would decrease greatly.

In large cities like New York, the fence may pose as an importer of precious gems. Legitimate merchants may buy from him without knowing that his stock consists of "hot" merchandise channeled to him by associates in other cities. Or he may be an established dealer who augments his stock with stolen merchandise which loses its identity. Such fences pay only a small fraction of the worth of the stolen goods, but the thieves aren't in a position to bargain.

Fencing has been described as a large-scale operation, international in scope. When criminal rings operate under cloak of legitimate business, they are very difficult to unmask and apprehend, particularly because it is so hard to identify individual diamonds. A particularly large or distinctive stone can be altered by a dishonest cutter, after which it is virtually impossible to trace.

13
Diamonds U. S. A.

There are whole veins of diamonds in thine eyes.
—P. J. Bailey

Wealthy in most mineral deposits, the United States was largely overlooked when diamonds were formed and scattered. A few fairly good-sized stones have been found in areas from New York to California, but there is nothing to indicate that profitable diamond-bearing fields exist anywhere in the country. A likely explanation is that the stones were picked up by glaciers during the Ice Age,

The Crater of Diamonds State Park in Murfreesboro, Arkansas, where finders are keepers. Credit: Little Rock State Parks Recreation and Travel Commission

carried long distances, and dropped when the glaciers receded. Thus there is no way to tell where the stones might have originated.

There is only one proven diamond-bearing area in all America to date. Near the town of Murfreesboro in Pike County, Arkansas, it has been certified as a genuine kimberlite pipe, about seventy-four acres in area. It has been given the fanciful name "Crater of Diamonds." Discovered in 1906, it was the object of a great deal of publicity and wishful promotion, but it never produced enough stones to justify full-scale commercial operations.

Various owners have held the property. Names like Henry Ford I and Glenn Martin, the aircraft builder, have been linked with it. Many hundreds of thousands of dollars reportedly have been spent in trying to develop the field. In 1942, according to one report, when the nation was badly in need of diamonds for production of war matériel, Arkansas Governor Homer Adkins, Senator Hattie Carraway, and two prominent New York jewelers called on President Franklin Roosevelt and showed him a case full of Arkansas diamonds. The report says that, in deference to the reputation of his visitors, Roosevelt ordered the War Production Board to entertain a priority for $500,000 in diamond mining machinery. The request eventually was turned down.

The largest diamond recovered in North America, called the Uncle Sam, was found in the Murfreesboro mine in 1924. Of good quality, it weighed in its rough state 40.23 carats. In cut form, it became the property of Peiken Jewelers of New York. Another stone, the Star of Arkansas, weighing 15.33 carats and also described as good quality, was found there in 1956 by Mrs. Arthur Parker of Dallas. A stone named the Punch Jones (34.46 carats) was found in 1928 at Peterstown, West Virginia, about 150 miles from the Murfreesboro pipe, whence it possibly originated. Another large stone was found by Mrs. P. Howard of Searcy, Arkansas, while working in a cotton field as a young girl. She picked up a shining pebble and kept it for twenty-one years before she realized

Mrs. Thomas W. Evener of Golden, Colorado, with a diamond she found.
Credit: The Nashville News, *Nashville, Arkansas*

that it might have value. It was eventually sent to Tiffany's, where it was declared to be a diamond of 27.21 carats.

As recently as the fall of 1971, a 5.5-carat stone was found at the Murfreesboro mine by Mrs. Marion Dell Evener of Golden, Colorado.

The pit is open to the public and finders are keepers. For a small fee, prospectors have access to the entire field and may search all day for diamonds. In 1972, the Crater of Diamonds was sold to the state of Arkansas, which plans to continue the operation as a tourist attraction and to develop adjacent land into a state park. This assures that the public will have access to the diamond-hunting grounds, an attraction that draws approximately 50,000 tourists a year.

My wife visited the mine several years ago and, while finding no diamonds, brought back some samples of kimberlite which she used in diamond lectures. What is regarded as the finest collection of American-found diamonds is housed in the Smithsonian Institution.

LARGEST ROUGH DIAMONDS FOUND IN THE UNITED STATES

Size (carats)	Name	Color	Where Found
40.23	Uncle Sam	White	Murfreesboro, Ark.
34.46	Punch Jones	Greenish	Peterstown, W. Va.
27.21	Arkansas (Searcy)	Cape	Searcy, Ark.
23.75	Dewey	White	Manchester, Va.
21.25	Theresa	Yellowish	Kohlsville, Wis.
20.25	Anon.	White	Murfreesboro, Ark.
18.20	Mounce	White	Princeton, La.
17.85	Arkansas Crystal	Yellow	Murfreesboro, Ark.
17.50	Morgantown	—	Morgantown, W. Va.
15.33	Star of Arkansas	White	Murfreesboro, Ark.
15.27	Eagle	Cape	Waukesha, Wis.
13.50	Chief of Carlisle	White	Murfreesboro, Ark.
12.50	Anon.	White	Syracuse, N.Y.
11.92	Cotton Belt Star	White	Murfreesboro, Ark.
10.87	Dowagiac	White	Cass Co., Mich.
7.50	Anon.	White	Jefferson Co., Ill.
7.25	French Coral	Yellowish	Nevada Co., Calif.
6.43	Garry Moore	White	Murfreesboro, Ark.
6.41	Saukville	White	Ozaukee Co., Wis.
6.00	Milford	White	Clermont Co., Ohio
5.50	Not yet named	White	Murfreesboro, Ark.
4.87	Stanley	Yellowish	Morgan Co., Ind.
4.50	Morrow	Yellowish	Clayton Co., Ga.
4.50	Lee	White	Lee Co., Ala.
4.33	Dyortsville	White	McDowell Co., N.C.
4.25	Birmingham	Yellow	Shelby Co., Ala.
4.00	Anon.	White	Brown Co., Ind.

Such is the lure of diamonds that two Kentuckians were able to perpetrate one of the greatest hoaxes of history. It happened in 1872, when imaginations had been sent soaring by the diamond discoveries in South Africa. The principals were Philip Arnold and John Slack, who had made a little money in the gold fields of California. Pooling their holdings of $75,000, Arnold went to London and purchased a quantity of rough diamonds, mostly of poor quality, and some other precious stones. These they scattered about in a desolate area later identified as northwestern Colorado.

Arnold and Slack then convinced a group of San Francisco bankers that they had discovered a fabulously rich diamond field and offered to guide them to it. The party traveled by train to southern Wyoming. To protect the secret of the field's location, Arnold and Slack blindfolded the bankers. It is not known how far they rode, but when the blindfolds were removed the bankers found themselves in a trackless wasteland that, wonder of wonders, seemed to abound with not only diamonds, but rubies, sapphires, and emeralds as well. The bankers hurried back to San Francisco and put some of the gems on display. Soon newspapers all over the West were hailing the news.

Beside themselves with excitement, the bankers called Henry Janin, a respected mining engineer and the chief mining consultant to the Bank of California. But even before Janin could be taken to the new Golconda, stock companies were formed. One, the San Francisco and New York Mining and Commercial Co., started with a capitalization of $10,000,000. The public clamored for stock at any price, but the incorporators decided this was too good a thing to share, and only two dozen men were permitted to invest up to $80,000 each.

Janin, blindfolded like the others, made the journey to the spot and was completely taken in. He hurried back with glowing reports to the bank. The news was cabled all over the world.

The Western bankers, convinced that the potential

"Off for the Diamond Fields"–an ad in the Mining and Scientific Press, *August 24, 1872. Credit: California State Library at Sacramento*

"*The Great Diamond Fields of America*"—*an article in the* Laramie Daily Independent, *August 19, 1872. Credit: Wyoming State Archives & Historical Department, Cheyenne*

was too big to be handled by themselves, went to New York to try to interest Eastern financiers. Some of New York's wealthiest men organized a syndicate. General George B. McClellan of Civil War fame, who had run against Lincoln for the presidency, was among the organizers. Samuel Barlow, one of the most influential lawyers of the day, joined the group and recommended the inclusion of General Benjamin F. Butler, who was a member of Congress and whose help would be needed to pass legislation to acquire the land involved in the diamond fields.

Despite their enthusiasm, the New Yorkers didn't allow their feelings to overcome caution. They insisted that another mining expert be sent to the diamond fields and that Tiffany & Co., which even then was a famous and respected jewelry firm, must examine and appraise the gems.

Charles Tiffany agreed. In Barlow's mansion, the men gathered secretly. A bag of stones was opened and the contents poured forth before the excited group. Tiffany methodically examined every stone, sorting them without haste into piles—the diamonds in one, the rubies in another, and the sapphires and emeralds in other orderly mounds.

Finally, he announced dramatically that they were indeed genuine. He wanted two days to check values with his lapidaries, but he stated that the stones were worth at least $150,000. The financiers were ecstatic.

Tiffany had seen only ten percent of the stones and, as it turned out, his valuation was ten times the true value of the gems. But, as there was little knowledge of rough diamonds in America at the time, he may be forgiven for his unwitting escalation of an already explosive situation. By the day's end, the meeting's secret had reached Wall Street. Investors begged to be allowed to buy stock and Tiffany was permitted to invest $80,000, the same as the incorporators.

Not all, of course, were caught up by the excitement. *The New York Times* printed a story casting doubt on the

"Arizona diamonds," as it described them, and expressed surprise that such men as Barlow and McClellan would allow their names to be tied up with such an enterprise. But few paid attention to the warning. The great London banking house of Rothschild purchased blocks of stock through its San Francisco branch. Other companies were formed over night, raising the capital involved to the amount of $250,000,000.

Meanwhile, Arnold expressed dissatisfaction with his contract involving $500,000. The bankers insisted that he had to accept the terms, suggested he was in company way over his head, and advised him to take the money and leave. He did both. Slack got $100,000 and also disappeared.

Meanwhile, geologist Clarence King, later to become the first head of the U. S. Geological Survey, made investigations of his own and came to the conclusion that the whole thing was a swindle. What raised his suspicions was the claim that diamonds, rubies, emeralds, and sapphires were found together. "The association of these minerals is a natural impossibility," he asserted.

Because the telegraph was under constant surveillance by hundreds of persons who wanted to learn the exact whereabouts of the diggings, he hurried by mule, horse, and finally by train to San Francisco, where he explained the facts to an amazed and chagrined group. The fraud was exposed without delay, thus saving thousands of speculators from financial disaster.

The story of the great diamond hoax inspired dozens of newspaper and magazine articles, chapters in many books, an eight-part story in the *Saturday Evening Post*, at least two books, and has been dramatized on television and radio. A hundred years after the event, it is still mentioned whenever diamond skulduggery is discussed.

14
Synthetic Gem Diamonds

Jade does not have . . . the glitter of diamonds.
—Tanizaki Junichiro in *Praise of Shadows*

I was stunned when the General Electric Company announced in May 1970 that it had succeeded in creating gem-quality diamonds. When a scientific feat like this is accomplished in your own backyard, so to speak, it seems to carry as much impact as achievements of far greater magnitude, like reaching the moon. On the second page of my previous book on diamonds, I had asserted that man had never succeeded in manufacturing gem-quality diamonds and implied that he never would. Obviously, I had underestimated man's scientific genius.

Anyway, on May 26, 1970, General Electric made its incredible statement.

Dr. Arthur M. Bueche, G.E. vice-president for research and development, said in making the announcement: "The creation of gem quality diamonds marks the exciting achievement of a goal that has tantalized and frustrated scientists for nearly two centuries."

G.E.'s first industrial diamonds in 1954 were sandlike grains. But once it was demonstrated that diamonds could be synthesized, the objective became larger specimens. By 1961, the company succeeded in making synthetic diamonds of size, but they were dark in color and structural imperfections deprived them of sufficient strength for some industrial applications. Because of the continuing need for large diamonds of good quality in industry, it was determined to keep the project going.

Dr. Herbert M. Strong and Dr. Robert H. Wentorf, two of the original team who synthesized diamonds at G.E. in

Dr. Herbert M. Strong, above, *and Dr. Robert H. Wentorf, Jr., the General Electric Company scientists who developed synthetic gem diamonds. Credit: General Electric Research and Development Center, the General Electric Company*

1954, persisted in their work, which had been marked by years of frustration, failures, and discouragement. The dogged persistence of the two men who never lost faith in the project until success rewarded them at last, makes a story which defies the imagination.

The process they perfected requires special apparatus able to withstand extreme pressures and temperatures for long periods of time. It starts with a tiny Man-Made—G.E.'s trade name for these stones—seed crystal no larger than the period at the end of this sentence. This is put into a press along with Man-Made diamond powder and a metal catalyst which are subjected to high pressures and temperatures under carefully controlled conditions.

The catalyst melts and the diamond powder dissolves, but a tube containing the diamond seed crystal is kept cool so it isn't damaged. Through these controlled temperatures and pressures, the carbon atoms from the diamond powder can be made to migrate through the catalyst and deposit themselves on the host crystal, forming a solid crystal lattice, much as salt or sugar crystals grow from water solutions. Gem-quality crystals of well over a carat and of various colors have been produced by the process.

Then the question arose as to how the crystals would behave under cutting and polishing stresses. Would they undergo these operations as well as natural crystals?

Just a year after the original announcement, General Electric through Dr. Bueche presented the Smithsonian Institution specimens of synthetic diamonds including three beautifully polished brilliants—one white, one blue, and the third canary—cut by the famous Lazare Kaplan and Sons. That put all doubts to rest. The presentation was an impressive ceremony behind closed doors of the Gem Wing of the museum, with Drs. Strong and Wentorf in attendance. The diamonds were impressive, indeed, in their illuminated case. It was an historic occasion, representing one of man's truly notable scientific achievements, and one I always shall remember.

When General Electric first announced the synthetic gem diamonds, it was stressed that they cost far more than natural diamonds and it was not known when, if ever, they would be marketed for public consumption. Company officials have emphasized they have no intention of disturbing the diamond world's economy.

In fact, at the Smithsonian presentation, one G.E. official showed me a large diamond he had just purchased

Victor and Margaret Argenzio view three gem diamonds made by the General Electric Company, in the Gem Room of the Smithsonian Institution. Credit: General Electric Research and Development Center, The General Electric Company

for his wife, indicating that he was not about to wait for his own company's possible emergence into the field of diamond sales.

However, the fact remains that the prototype of anything is the most costly. There may come a time when synthetic diamonds might be made economically enough to be put on the market if G.E. wishes. How would they affect the value of natural stones? There is no answer at this time, but the record shows that the introduction of synthetic star sapphires, rubies, and cultured emeralds helped rather than hurt the values of genuine stones.

As long as the Man-Made diamonds can be identified by Gem Laboratories as such, which seems assured, they should find their own price level, which probably will be quite a bit lower than natural and a good deal more than the

Dr. Arthur M. Bueche, vice-president of General Electric–Research and Development Division, with the author in the Smithsonian Institution's Gem Room. Credit: General Electric Research and Development Center, the General Electric Company

present-day imitations, the best of which are much softer than natural diamonds. I see no threat from Man-Made diamonds to the owners of the natural gems.

15
Offbeat

What art thou, that counterfeits the person of a king?
—Shakespeare, *King Henry IV*, Part 1, Act V, Scene 4

DIAMOND IMITATIONS

Imitation diamonds have been made for centuries.

Caderousse, the famed thief in Dumas' *The Count of Monte Cristo* (1845), came across some in a jewelry store robbery and uttered these priceless words: "Those thieves of jewelers imitate so well that it is no longer profitable to rob a jewelry store. It is another branch of industry paralyzed."

New and better imitations have been created in recent years, many of which got into the hands of crooks who pawned or tried to pawn them off as the real thing. I purchased some samples and found that, while they wouldn't fool knowledgeable persons, they could deceive the uninitiated. In an effort to alert the public, *The Denver Post* published an interview with me under the headline "Fake Diamonds Not Buyer's Best Friend." *The New York Times* reprinted *The Post* article.

Then the story took an unexpected twist. One of the distributors of these fake diamonds picked up *The Post* interview and used it in his advertising, pointing out proudly that it took an expert to distinguish his product from genuine diamonds. Like other makers of imitations, he frankly advertised them as fakes, and, of course, there's nothing wrong with that. But when an unknown individual offers a "diamond bargain," be on guard.

There are many types of imitation diamonds, including

synthetic white sapphires and synthetic spinel. In 1953, an imitation made of strontium titanate was introduced. This type of stone has a high degree of fire and brilliance. However, on the widely used Mohs scale of hardness, it measures only 5 to 6, which is soft enough to be scratched by ordinary kitchen cleansers. The diamond rates 10 on the Mohs scale.

A more recent development is a product known as YAG, for synthetic yttrium aluminum garnet. It rates 8.25 on the Mohs hardness scale, which gives it somewhat better wearing qualities. The drawback of YAG is that it isn't so brilliant as the strontium titanate products, nor does it as closely resemble a diamond.

The Mohs scale of hardness was devised in 1812 by a German mineralogist. Based on scratching power, it ranks various substances in a graded series according to which will scratch another. The shortcoming of the scale is that it doesn't measure the difference in hardness between the numbers. The scale ranks talc, extremely soft, number 1. Quartz is rated 7. Topaz, which can scratch quartz, gets an 8 classification. The difference in hardness between 7 and 8 is not great, but there is a tremendous gap between 9, which includes corundum (ruby and sapphire), and 10, the diamond, which is 140 times harder than corundum.

So when the ads read, as they often do, "Our product is almost as hard as diamond, Mohs rating of 8.50 to diamond's 10," they are by no stretch of the imagination in a similar class.

New kinds of imitation diamonds appear on the market regularly. One folder recently sent to me advertises a 4-carat stone set in a 14K gold mounting for half the price that a 1-carat loose YAG sold for when they were first merchandised. Another manufacturer offers a loose stone which sells for $2 per carat. It makes one wonder how much cheaper some of these imitations will become. Such stones have their place in junk jewelry, but certainly not in engagement rings. Not everyone can afford a Rembrandt and, many must settle, at best, for a print, but most of us can afford a real diamond, which imparts a warmth and pride of ownership that has no counterpart in any other gem. Better a small diamond than a large fake.

COLOR CHANGE

Because by far the greatest majority of diamonds have a yellow or brown tinge of varying degree, attempts to improve their color have been going on for more than a century. The improvement, if any, is always temporary. The new color often lasts not much longer than the consummation of the sale. Needless to say, the object of these efforts is to fool an unwary bargain hunter. Such altered stones are never seen in the stores of ethical merchants. The methods used are as crude as coloring the girdle (the extreme outside edge of stone) with blue ink or blue pencil. Stones also have been soaked in blue-tinted chemicals to coat them with a very thin film. In older times, diamonds sometimes had foil backs applied to the lower half of the stones to improve brilliancy. These are occasionally found today in old pieces of jewelry. The backs of these stones are always closed. Even today a diamond backed with gold foil is justifiably suspect.

Different from these practices of temporarily improving the shade of a diamond is the complete changing of color of diamonds from an off-white, yellow, or brown into more desirable blue, green, canary, and other colors by ir-radiation. The objective is to upgrade gems of inferior color.

Scientists have learned that most diamonds contain nitrogen atoms and that the arrangement of these atoms governs color. In some way, radioactive waves affect the nitrogen atoms. It was discovered many years ago that radium treatment gave diamonds a greenish tinge. However, this treatment produced some hazardous re-sidual radioactivity.

Then it was found that color could be changed by bombarding diamonds in a cyclotron with subatomic particles that create centers which absorb certain wavelengths of light. When this happens, the light (color) which emerges is different from that entering. This method produces the blues and greens; with additional treatment, other colors are obtained. With this system, the colors are permanent, if the stones are not subjected to a further high degree of heat.

Occasionally a green or blue-green stone has been known to fade. The heat and stress generated in recutting an irradiated diamond also may affect the color. Irradiated diamonds may even change color when a ring is being sized by a jewelry repairman not familiar with this type of stone. In answer to my query about irradiated diamonds, the eminent Swiss gemologist, Charles A. Schiffmann, wrote: "In fact it sounds like a paradox, but it is true that the nature of a fancy colored diamond, whether natural or treated, can be asserted by heating the diamond. If the color does not change, the color is natural. Of course, this is a rather drastic and dangerous test."

The way a stone is cut seems to have a bearing on how it takes to irradiation. Round and emerald cuts are best for color change. Marquise and pear shapes do not lend themselves so well for the process; owing to absorption limitations, part of the stones of these shapes come out a little lighter shade than the body of the stone.

Irradiated diamonds are not as brilliant as stones of natural color. Dr. Frederick Pough, a noted American gemological authority, explains: "It must be remembered that color is caused by the absorption of part of the incident white light, consequently no colored diamond can be as brilliant as its colorless counterpart. On the other hand, it will be more brilliant than like-hued colored stones."

The Federal Trade Commission has ruled that irradiated diamonds must be identified as such, but the regulation is not always observed. Some years ago, after I was quoted in a newspaper article about bombarded diamonds, a wealthy industrialist came to me with a large green diamond. He said he had bought it at an auction of the estate of Major Bowes, a well-known radio personality. The bill of sale listed the stone as a natural green diamond, but he wanted to be certain.

I couldn't tell for sure, so the stone was sent to the Gemological Institute of America, the nation's foremost authority. It came back with the verdict: "Color due to irradiation."

More recently a large golden yellow diamond, purported to be the famous Deepdene diamond which weighs over 100 carats, was auctioned in Geneva. A bid of almost $500,000 was made by one of Europe's most famous jewelers. Because the amount involved was large, the jeweler had the stone checked by the world-famous Swiss gemologist, Dr. Edward Gübelin, and the equally-famed Briton, B. W. Anderson. They both stated the stone had been irradiated and that it was not the true Deepdene, which is of natural color. Subsequently, it was sent to the Gemological Institute of America, where our own expert, G. Robert Crowningshield, concurred. So the transaction was never consummated.

There is nothing wrong with buying an irradiated diamond if you want a fancy color and don't mind it being produced by man. Such stones cost much less than a comparable stone of the same natural color. But you should know it if a stone has been irradiated.

REMOVING BLACK SPOTS

A new wrinkle, removing black spots from diamonds, is in operation in some shops in the United States and abroad.

The method is to burn a tiny hole into the diamond by use of a laser beam. First, the laser machine draws a bead on the flaw through a special microscope. Then, with several short bursts of energy ranging to thousands of times per second, a hole is burned to the black flaw, which is eliminated. If the cavity is not whitened entirely, it is bleached with one of several special volatile liquids. A very tiny hole remains, no larger than 1/1000 inch. As the means of operations improve, it is reported that the hole has diminished in some cases to 1/10,000 inch, and the whitening process must be accomplished by use of fumes of the acids.

These holes are difficult to find even under high magnification.

France was the first nation to rule that such diamonds must be described as treated stones and that the buyer must be told they are so treated. The U. S. Federal Trade Commission probably will pick up such a ruling eventually.

16
Diamonds at Work

Fetch a sack of black diamonds from the wharf.
—Thomas Miller in *Garboni in London*

When diamonds are mentioned, gems come to mind first, but a far more important role is played by them in the world of industry and science. The industrial world as we know it would not be possible without them; diamonds make possible miracles of science and our trips to the moon.

Nature must have had an idea of the importance they would assume because, of all diamonds mined, eighty percent are of industrial quality and only twenty percent qualify as gems. Even so, synthetic industrial diamonds must supplement nature's output to meet today's ever-increasing needs. The diamond's hardness is the key to its many applications in industry. The diamond's cutting qualities are a great boon to users of hard alloys and heat-resisting materials. Not only is a high degree of precision possible with diamonds, but they also give faster working speeds and longer life to tools.

The use of diamonds as industrial tools was known 2500 years ago, when Chinese and Indian lapidaries used them to polish jade and other gems. In the fifteenth century, it was found that diamonds could be ground into powder which, when mixed with olive oil, became an excellent medium for cutting and grinding. A few years later, diamonds were used in a primitive sort of rock drill.

As man's industrial skills improved, so did the ways in which diamonds were used—to draw wire in the early nineteenth century, for drilling and engraving, in the grinding of microscopic lenses. The diamond saw, a most

Two diamond-bladed Bumpcutters work in tandem and offset from one another grooving Interstate 35W in South Minneapolis. Each machine has 17 diamond blades mounted on a rotating shaft. Credit: Peter Silveri and Assoc.

The BART system will be the most advanced in the United States, possibly in the world. Diamonds played an important part in various phases of construction. Credit: DeBeers Industrial Diamond Division

important tool, made its appearance in 1854. A few years later, diamond drills helped construct the Mount Cenis Alpine tunnel. As metals replaced wood, the foundation was laid for precision engineering and diamonds became indispensable.

For purposes such as dies for wire drawing, diamonds without flaws must be used. For the most part, diamonds which are poor in color but of good internal structure are typed for this work. Billions of miles of wire are drawn annually through diamond dies.

A cone-shaped hole is drilled through the diamond, which is set in a steel or bronze plate. The wire is pulled through dies of progressively smaller diameters until the wire is finer than human hair. Many thousands of miles of wire can be drawn through a diamond before the hole shows signs of wear. Then the hole is reshaped into the next larger size. When, at last, the stone can no longer be redrilled, it is ground to powder and used for other purposes.

This picture telephone, now being manufactured and used, would not be possible without a special type of diamond. Credit: Mountain Bell Telephone Co.

For rock drilling, natural diamonds of various sizes—some as large as 4 or 5 carats—are mounted in rotating steel bits which chew their way into the earth in the quest for oil and minerals or into mountainsides in boring tunnels.

The poorest, smallest, least expensive, most unglamorous diamonds are called bort. Crushed and powdered, they are used in grinding wheels and saws. They comprise by far the greatest amount of diamond material used. Diamond wheels represent the major use in metal working; in fact, metal working applications account for 20,000,000 carats of the total annual consumption of approximately 55,000,000 carats.

Always important in peacetime, diamonds are particularly indispensable on the home production front in wartime.

In World War II, a shortage of industrials threatened the Allied forces. When Belgium and Holland were overrun, diamonds were among the first items to be rushed to safety. One result was that technologies arising from the war entrenched diamond abrasives became an essential part of modern production methods.

These are 10,000 ton presses used to synthesize diamonds. Credit: DeBeers Industrial Diamond Division

During the action in Korea, natural sources again were inadequate for the demands made on them. As is so often the case, man's ingenuity was equal to the occasion—and synthetics were born.

Attempts to synthesize diamonds go back more than a century. The first to receive worldwide interest was the claim of Hannay, a Scottish chemist, in 1880. A few years later a French scientist, Moissan, claimed that he, too, had been successful in producing synthetic diamonds. These claims have remained in doubt. Most authorities agree that the first proven success was accomplished in 1953 by the great Swedish combine known as A. S. E. A. No one can understand why the firm didn't announce or patent its findings, but it did not do so. We do know that world patents were issued to General Electric in 1955. G. E.'s experimental work was started in 1951, when the Korean War's industrial needs underscored the importance of industrial diamonds. The company's first diamonds were so tiny that 1000 were needed to equal a single carat. Efforts to make larger and better specimens finally resulted in synthetic gem diamonds of good sizes.

The construction of the side wall of a canal in France. The concrete paving train (right) is being followed by a battery of diamond saws (left) sawing contraction joints. Credit: DeBeers Industrial Diamond Division

For many purposes, some synthetic material has proven superior to mined diamonds. This is because their properties may be controlled and tailored for specific uses. Such giants as DeBeers are now actively engaged in the production of synthetics, for which new uses are continually being discovered. The world's largest diamond research laboratory in Johannesburg is devoted to finding new and better uses of diamonds, both natural and synthetic.

What is the total consumption of industrial diamonds? In 1939, 5,000,000 carats—all natural—went into industry. In 1971, approximately 55,000,000 carats, natural and synthetic, were absorbed by industry.

The growth rate is estimated to be ten percent per year as new uses are found for working diamonds. A natural diamond may provide the cutting edge of a knife

Grinding wheels come in many widths, diameters, and shapes. They are used to machine many super hard materials. Credit: DeBeers Industrial Diamond Division, Peter Silveri and Associates

for sectioning biological tissues for electron microscopic examination; another diamond may be set in a tool for resurfacing bowling balls.

Interest in new uses for diamonds is worldwide and recognizes no limitations of distance. For example, *The New York Times* tells American readers about Italian quarrymen shifting from saws which used sand as an abrasive to diamond-tipped ones, which are indescribably superior.

In a South African magazine, we read of diamond-bladed cutters grooving the concrete of an interstate highway in Minnesota.

A diamond scriber etching intricate designs on a Swedish glass bowl. Credit: DeBeers Industrial Diamond Division

A British trade publication runs a detailed story on the use of diamonds in the construction of BART, the San Francisco Bay Area Rapid Transit system.

From Denmark comes news of a "naked" diamond stylus for maximum wear in a stereophonic record player. I read once that a diamond phonograph needle, set at random, played for 600 hours continuously, and, when the "hard" direction of the diamond was presented, it was still performing well after 2500 hours. The crystal structure of a diamond gives it hard and soft directions, and this,

During World War II, the War Production Board deemed these industrial diamonds so necessary that their sale and delivery were put under government control. Credit: Wide World Photo

apparently, is what the Danes are telling us. Of course, even the soft direction of a diamond is extremely hard.

A rare type of industrial diamond, known as type IIa and found principally at the Premier mine in Pretoria, South Africa, has the unique quality of heat conductivity, which makes it ideal for use in the electronic industry. Researchers are uncovering other ways to utilize its characteristics.

It will have a part in developing picture telephone systems, radar navigation systems for small ships, directional radar for small planes, computerized radar for docking the world's largest passenger and cargo vessels, and numerous other electronic devices.

Sometimes industrial diamonds are cast in dramatic roles. When a workman was trapped deep in a Utah mine, rescuers knew they could never reach him in time with ordinary drills. But when a huge diamond-tipped drill arrived, it chewed its way quickly through rock and in a short time the man was rescued.

Without diamonds, many machine-age mass production processes would come to a stop as surely as though the power were shut off. A friend who recently visited our home was asked: "Are industrial diamonds important to your factory?" He replied: "Without diamonds, we'd come to a screeching halt!"

Gem diamonds have been known through the ages as a girl's best friend. In a sense, they may be compared to luxury liners, which win admiration and acclaim. Industrial diamonds are like ocean freighters, which perform the essential and often unglamorous services without fanfare. But who can say that industrial diamonds are not a man's best friend?

17

Diamonds for Men

. . . the best of us here have more of rough than polished diamond.
—Earl of Chesterfield, letters to his son, 1848

When the French king, Francis I, wasn't fighting Charles V in some war or other in the sixteenth century, he had his lighter moments. It is said that he spent much time scratching amorous messages on palace windows with his favorite sharp-pointed diamond ring. His contemporary, Henry VIII of England (the one with the wives), had a few diamond rings himself, as well as a set of 500 diamond buttons which he wore at the same time to cover his generous girth and to impress the French monarch.

Long before, in the eighth century, Charlemagne had an octahedron-shaped diamond (they weren't cut or faceted in those days) set in a yellow gold ring.

Hundreds of years later, Diamond Jim Brady, like Francis I, used one of his diamond rings to scratch windowpanes.

Diamonds were something of a curiosity to many in the United States in the 1880s. Diamond Jim, a locomotive salesman, was able to get many hard-to-come-by appointments with railroad magnates because they were anxious to see his diamond collection. While he discussed railroad equipment, he also displayed his assortment of diamonds, capping the show by striding to the nearest window and writing his name, James Buchanan Brady, on the glass with a diamond. His signature on an office window came to be considered a status symbol.

Good taste wasn't Jim's forte, however. His rings contained stones of enormous size and his jewelry was set with as many diamonds as possible, but with little attention to artistic design. Although diamonds made him wealthy, Jim Brady unwittingly had a hand in making men's diamonds unpopular.

When I started working in a jewelry store, diamond rings for men were again becoming popular. The first sale of a diamond of any kind which I made was to a man who had purchased several diamond rings and several pieces of diamond jewelry for his wife. He now wanted a ring for himself.

Men mostly buy diamonds for women, but more and more men are buying one for themselves. These days, they are worn in rings and enjoyed by every class of men. Some regard them as a success symbol, like a fine car. Some men wear diamonds because they are a negotiable cash asset. Mainly, however, men wear diamond rings because they like them.

Sentiment is attached to many diamonds. Countless times I have seen a man who inherited his father's diamond ring bring it in to have it checked for security or for a more modern setting. Often a diamond ring is purchased by the wife who is aware of her husband's secret wish for one. Sometimes it works the other way.

One man brought in his deceased wife's diamond ring and asked that the stone be set in a mounting he could wear. "That way I shall always have one of her most treasured possessions close to me," he said.

Not everyone agrees with me that men should wear diamonds if they choose to. Walter Hoving, as chairman of Tiffany and Company, in a speech to the New York Society of Security Analysts said in part: "Now, I hope none of you gentlemen is wearing a diamond ring, because if you are, you didn't buy it at Tiffany's. You must have gotten it elsewhere. We do not carry diamond rings for men. I suppose we throw away some business in that area, too. But we say quite frankly, 'We are sorry, sir, but we don't think it attractive for a man to wear a diamond ring. If you want one, you will have to go elsewhere.' "

I took issue with him publicly and my views were widely published. Professor Carlyle H. Smith, head of the Department of Jewelry and Silversmithing at the University of Kansas, has remarked: "A well-designed diamond ring can complement the wearer, be it man or woman. Too large a diamond, or too many diamonds, can be vulgar unless great care is taken by the designer. I am afraid that Mr. Hoving does not give the male of the species, in general, enough credit for common sense regarding his appreciation of good taste."

I believe Professor Smith speaks for the majority. Men's rings definitely are gaining in popularity. Statistics show that ten years ago one man's ring was sold for every ten women's rings; today the ratio is 1 to 2.5.

It is only fitting, I feel, that men, who mine, cut, and sell diamonds, who utilize them in industry to give us the benefits of their technology, also should have the right to enjoy them in their personal jewelry.

18

My Life with Diamonds:
A Compilation of Reminiscences
and Personal Observations

*There's always something a little anticlimactic about the
Christmas gift that arrives too late . . . unless, of course, it's a
diamond . . . and then it's Christmas whenever it gets there.*
—Virginia Payette, in the Denver Rocky Mountain News

My first job was in a Denver jewelry store. I was sixteen.
For $6 per week, I swept the floor and dusted the
showcases. But my main interest was in the diamonds
displayed in those showcases. I was so intrigued by them
that I studied them at every opportunity. Soon I was able
to tell the real from the imitations; there weren't many
variations of the latter in those days, which made it easier.

One day, a man talked my boss into giving him a job
as an experienced jewelry salesman. He was domineering
and unpleasant. I was just a kid, but soon it became
evident to me that he knew nothing about our business.

When a customer left a diamond ring with me for
repair one day, I took it to him and told a little lie: "Miss
Wendell [a knowledgeable senior clerk] says this is not a
diamond, while I am sure it is. What is it?" He looked at it
through his magnifying eye loupe and replied, "Of course
it isn't a diamond. But don't feel bad, you'll learn some
day." When I reported the incident to the boss, the faker
was fired.

In one of my capacities as errand boy, I became
acquainted with both ethical and nonethical diamond
retailers. The shady ones made my job a delight, and I

looked forward to making deliveries to shops where unorthodox practices were frequent. I remember one dealer who was trying to make a sale to a customer who apparently didn't believe the diamond was exactly as represented and finally asked for a written guarantee. The dealer agreed readily, made it out, and said to the buyer: "Here it is, just sign here." And darned if the chap didn't sign his own name to it!

Another incident has to do with a jeweler who liked to boast that no customer ever left his store with as much money as he had when he walked in. I observed him trying to sell a young soldier a necklace containing a very tiny diamond. The price was $30. The youngster simply wasn't interested, but the jeweler was determined to sell the item. Gradually he lowered the price to $15. When the boy still said no, the merchant wrapped up the necklace and said, "Look, buddy, you have fought for your country and my country. To show you my appreciation, you are going to get this beautiful necklace for only $12.50." With that, he handed over the jewelry to the soldier. Somewhat taken aback, the lad accepted the package and left the store poorer than when he entered. But at $12.50 he got good value, I thought.

In time, I became a junior clerk. My salary was raised to $8 per week and for the first time, I was allowed to sell diamonds. My first sale was a 1-carat diamond ring priced at several hundred dollars. This hooked me forever to the world of diamonds and resulted in my salary being raised again—to $10 per week. In addition, the boss presented me with a stickpin set with a tiny diamond. It is still a treasured possession.

But in my first year of selling diamonds there were also some disturbing incidents. One time, after a prospective customer left, one of the rings I had shown him was missing. I fearfully told my boss who, I was sure, would end my affair with diamonds then and there. But he didn't. Patiently he explained once again that too much caution can't ever be exercised in a jewelry store.

A week or so later, when I came in from lunch, there

was the same man looking at more rings at the same case where I had been. I watched him like a hawk, ready to give the alarm if he tried anything suspicious. During a moment when the clerk's attention was distracted, he reached down under the bottom of the showcase. Instinctively, I dashed toward him. When he saw me, with one motion he threw something at me and fled from the store. What he had thrown was the missing ring covered with chewing gum. Undoubtedly he had taken advantage of my inexperience to hide the ring, planning to retrieve it later.

In 1925, my brother Joseph and I started in business for ourselves in Denver. Joseph had experience in dealing with diamonds, so he did the buying and grading while I admired them and occasionally sold one.

The first few years were difficult. After it looked as though we were getting on our feet, the Great Depression hit. Business vanished. The values we were able to offer were exceptional, but there were few takers.

One of our more memorable sales was a platinum watch set with many diamonds. We had sold it for $50, but it just didn't run well. Finally, the lady who had purchased it came in and demanded her money back. Well, we didn't have $50 at the moment, but my brother saved the day—and the business—by persuading her to give us another chance with it. He pointed out that a watch is a piece of machinery which occasionally needs a few adjustments before it runs properly.

For example, he said, even a new Packard car, one of the great ones then, sometimes needed some corrections to get it operating just right. Well, our business was not destined for doom that day. The customer had bought a Packard car a few weeks previously, had some trouble at first, and now it was running smoothly. So we were given another chance with the watch.

One day, feeling very discouraged about things in general and the jewelry business in particular, I wrote to A. P. Giannini, chairman of the Bank of America, for advice. Even though I didn't know him, I asked whether we should continue the struggle with what seemed an unnecessary type of business or start over in something more practical, like selling hamburgers.

Giannini replied in a two-page letter stating that he thought the jewelry business was very necessary to the economy because of its connotations of the happy things in life, especially during times of stress such as we were all undergoing. He urged us to stick with it.

Despite the letter of encouragement, my spirits continued to sag along with the ever-worsening business conditions. Finally, when I found that my health was being affected, I decided to borrow money and take a trip to Europe and the Near East. I had become anything but an asset for our firm and I wanted a change so I could regain my perspective.

In Rome, I found a room with a private family. It cost just a fraction of a hotel rate. When it was learned that I was a jeweler, two members of the family asked my opinion about a ring, a family heirloom. Locking the door and drawing the curtains, they rummaged through a closet and came out with a worn jewelry box. Then the whole family—all eight of them—gathered round me in great anticipation. The ring was a very old one. Often such heirlooms prove to be of little value, but I was happy to be able to assure them that they actually had a real diamond, though not a very valuable one. They were delighted and the rest of my stay was made so pleasant that I hated to leave.

After a few months, my health was fully restored and my borrowed money was running low, so I returned home with a new outlook on life which has lasted me to the present. Business conditions slowly started to improve and I found a real joy in selling—diamonds especially. Then, just before the all-important sales month of December, my brother suffered a heart attack. Fortunately, it was not a serious one, but, as it was he who understood and graded the diamonds, I trembled at the thought of taking over the responsibility. We were starting to acquire a reputation for diamonds and I realized I understood very little about their quality. It was obvious that more than my love for these gems was going to be needed.

The spring after Joseph returned to work, I took a short resident course on diamonds at the Los Angeles branch of the Gemological Institute of America. Subsequently I made it a practice to examine and analyze every diamond we purchased, and I slowly learned. Then I took the mail order course which G.I.A. puts out, and diamonds began to acquire a very real personality. I began reading everything I could find about them, eventually wrote and spoke about them, and became more enthused than ever with what I have always considered the world's greatest gem.

I also learned a great deal about people. A jewelry store attracts a wide cross-section of humanity, with its mixture of weaknesses and nobility, and there is something about a jeweler's showcase which often reveals a person's real character.

I was impressed at the beginning of my career by the great pleasure that diamonds give people—to the donors as well as the recipients. A man buying a fine piece of diamond jewelry for his wife doesn't complain about her; he extolls her attributes and wishes he could afford an even finer piece for her.

I never tire of the thrill of helping a young couple select their engagement and wedding rings. Even when they try to conceal their emotions, the transaction is a source of delight to a dedicated jeweler. The betrothal diamond is a symbol of the start of many exciting, pleasurable events. To share the couple's bliss vicariously, even if only in a small way, is a most rewarding experience.

Of course, not all couples are like this. I have seen arguments over the selection of the ring. And when, occasionally, members of the families of the pair are present, taking a strong position against the wishes of one or the other, it is obvious that there will be rough going ahead. After many years, a jeweler is almost certain he can tell which marriages will be successful and which will be doomed by selfishness, immaturity, or outside interference.

Often I have sold diamonds to older women who have never married. Their story is the same: "I am not one of the fortunate ones who have had a diamond given to me. If I'm to have one, I am going to have to buy it personally. But I am not going to miss out on the joy of owning a diamond."

Middle-aged men, after achieving some financial success, will buy their wives a larger diamond than they could afford at first. Sometimes the original stone is traded in for a larger or finer diamond. Occasionally, the wife keeps the original, full of happy memories, and has it mounted in a pendant or other piece of jewelry.

I have sold diamond rings to many an elderly widow after her children were grown and married. The story is a familiar one. The husband could not afford a "good" diamond while struggling to raise and educate the children. Now, with the husband gone, the widow uses some of the money he left her to buy the gem he had always wanted her to have.

I know one young doctor—he is middle-aged now—who kept trading in stones he bought his wife through the years, until now she proudly wears a huge diamond, something they wanted but couldn't afford at first.

But one also encounters different stories: the chap who buys a beautiful piece for a girlfriend while purchasing a bit of costume jewelry for his wife; the switch artist who tries to exchange an imitation for a good diamond; and the innumerable variations of the bunco artists.

Not long ago, one such crook showed a prospect a tray containing eight platinum diamond rings. The price for the lot was ridiculously low, and it was explained that they were from a distressed jeweler's stock.

The prospect was taken to two different jewelers,

both of whom identified the stones as genuine. But after the man bought the rings, he found the stones were imitations. They were brought into our store by police for identification; the crook had prepared two sets of identical rings, one set with real diamond centers.

Diamonds have been good to me. I never made a fortune buying and selling them, but I have had many marvelous things happen because of them. When a man brings in his son, as frequently happens to an old-time jeweler, and says, "Take care of him as you did me twenty-five years ago," it makes us realize that we have established the kind of reputation that cannot be purchased.

Some years ago the physician for the San Francisco '49ers football team sent me his wife's mounting, from which a good sized diamond had been lost, together with a blank check and a three-word note: "Fill in both." These are rewarding incidents, indeed, and I don't mean only financially.

One of my first ventures into writing was an article on diamonds for Consumer's Research. This led to others. I was especially thrilled when the Federal Trade Commission asked me to write an article on how to buy a diamond, and what to avoid when buying.

My first book, *The Fascination of Diamonds*, brought me wonderful, friendly letters from all over the country. A British edition brought glowing letters from many countries. My book wasn't all that good, but what pleased me was the interest people show in diamonds.

Diamonds have enabled my wife and me to travel—to the South African diamond mines and to such diamond centers as Antwerp and Israel.

An interesting sidelight to our trip in Israel was a ride from Tel-Aviv to Haifa. I had seen Haifa in the early 1930s and wanted to see what changes had taken place. In a few words, what was formerly a dirty, unbelievably unkempt city is now possibly the garden spot of Israel. Our driver pointed out how his nation is surrounded by enemy countries and went on to say he thought that hostilities might break out at any time. A few weeks later, the Six-Day War of 1967 took place.

On the same trip, a letter of introduction from Colonel George Visser, then security head of DeBeers, opened doors to the Topkapi Museum in Istanbul and gave my wife and me a chance to examine its marvelous treasures. We were even permitted to handle the dagger which was made famous in the motion picture *Topkapi*.

I couldn't help comparing this visit to Istanbul to the

An Arab potentate with a diamond toothpick. Credit: Mile High Photo

one I made on my trip during the Depression. That time, I left the Topkapi Museum in a cab for my ship. I was nearly out of Turkish money, so I gave a $5 bill to the cabby. He took one look and he came at me with a wicked-looking knife. I grabbed the money and fled. Well, a man with a knife pointed at him can outrun the man holding it, so I escaped.

A year later, while talking to another American who had traveled in Turkey, I learned what had happened. He roared with laughter when I told him of my experience. Then he explained that when he was stationed in Istanbul as a sailor, he and some of his friends had paid for tickets for shows and other amusements, including the local sporting houses, with cigar coupons. Later the Turks learned to recognize George Washington's face and accepted U. S. dollar bills from Americans. So when I presented a bill with Abe Lincoln's face on it, the cabby must have thought I was an American up to old tricks.

The second time in Istanbul a special car returned my wife and me to our hotel. Time and circumstances do change.

Our next stop was Vienna, where I asked the concierge for two tickets for that night's performance of *The Magic Flute* by Mozart. The concierge smiled sadly and said the Statsoper had been sold out for weeks.

That evening, just as we had ordered dinner, the man rushed to our table with the news that he had been able to gather two tickets for Magic Flute after all. I said, "Impossible. We won't have time to change, get a cab, and get Austrian money." He slapped down the two tickets plus several dollars worth of schillings, and cried: "Rush, the cab is waiting downstairs." Surely this could happen only at the Am Stephansplatz Hotel.

We arrived at 7:32 P. M. The opera in Vienna starts at 7:30. My wife and I had to separate as the tickets were not together. I was whisked upstairs to a box where I received somewhat less than friendly looks. The reason I tell this story at all is that one of the occupants of the box had taken an extraordinary cigarette case from his pocket while looking for something else.

At the intermission, when we had all become acquainted, I asked to see his case. It was the most elaborate cigarette container I had ever seen. The top must have been set with a hundred or more diamonds, some of them large, fancy-cut stones. The case was a heavy gold one with the stones set in platinum. At least it looked like platinum. The man's name sounded Persian. I volunteered that his diamond cigarette box must be the world's most valuable and by rights should be on display with the other fabulous Iranian jewels. He smiled and nodded.

Subsequently we went to Amsterdam, where we were greeted by Louis Asscher at his diamond-cutting plant. Mr. Asscher is the nephew of the famous Joseph Asscher, who cleaved the great Cullinan. Then on to London where, in addition to my visit to one of the famous "sights" where the distribution of the rough diamonds starts, my wife and I were accorded the unusual honor of a private showing of the British Crown Jewels. Getting close to the Kohinoor, the Cullinans, and the other great jewels on display in the Tower of London was an indescribable thrill.

On our trip from London to Dublin, there was a mix-up in the tickets. For the first time in our 25,000-mile journey, my wife and I didn't have plane seats together. I sat next to a large distinguished-looking man. We introduced ourselves briefly. I didn't catch his name, and as the trip would be a short one, it didn't matter.

I told him I was a jeweler on my way back from the diamond mines in South Africa. He said he was in the publishing business. When I showed interest in the jewelry trade magazines which he published, he promised to mail some to me. Endeavoring to hold up my end of the conversation, I tried to impress him by stating that I was having a book about diamonds published in New York. He kindly answered that if I mailed a copy to him he would show it to his various editors and, if any liked the book, it might be possible to arrange for a British edition. Sometime later he mentioned that he had recently purchased *The London Times.*

My neighbor was courteous and most pleasant. He was obviously an important man, but I couldn't help thinking that he was just trying to impress me, and when he mentioned the *Times* I was sure of it. Then he referred to his watch.

This, I thought, seemed a little unusual, so I asked to see it. On the dial was an inscription in Arabic, and on the back was engraved, "To Lord Thomson from King Feisal"! "As a matter of fact," said my neighbor, who suddenly assumed huge proportions, "I think I'm giving the chap a banquet shortly." Referring to his notebook he said, "Yes, here it is" (showing me). "Banquet for King Feisal, 20 April."

When I got home, there were the promised copies of the magazines along with a letter from Eric Bruton, the editor of one of them and the author of the recently published comprehensive book *Diamonds.* The letter stated that he had been at a banquet with His Lordship, who had mentioned having a very enjoyable conversation with me. I must confess that I got quite a kick out of being able to tell the distinguished Lord Thomson of Fleet that arrangements had already been completed with a London firm (George Allen and Unwin) to publish my book there. One of Life's Great Moments.

In 1971, on a trip to the Far East, I observed at first hand a bit of the diamond activities in Japan, Hong Kong, and other places. In Tokyo, an English-speaking Japanese girl who was selling me some film was wearing a ring with a good-sized stone. When I asked to see it, she became somewhat embarrassed, and before I could examine it closely, she volunteered that it was one of the new fakes. Et tu, Brute!

Also in 1971, I was invited by G. E.'s Dr. Bueche to view the presentation of the first cut Man-Made gem diamonds, which I described in an earlier chapter.

In 1972, I was given the unusual and great honor of

being the only jeweler judge at the American Diamond Competition in New York. This made me feel that, while I have retired from the scene of active business, I am still part of the great diamond world, and nothing can make me happier.

PART II

Diamonds and You

How to evaluate, buy, enjoy, and safeguard the most delightful of all gems

1

Buying a Diamond

The purchase of a diamond, especially your first, can be a very pleasurable and rewarding experience. It also can be a trying one, if only because the average person knows surprisingly little about what factors determine a diamond's value and what to look for in shopping for one.

Due to demand, diamonds now are found for sale in many places other than established jewelry stores. This leads inevitably to sellers of precious objects who know little more, if anything, than the purchaser. The best guarantee of getting proper value for the money spent on a diamond is to buy the stone from an established and reliable jeweler. He has devoted many years to building up his knowledge and reputation, and these are his greatest assets. He will be the first to tell you there are few bargains in diamonds, and that you usually get what you pay for. He also will help you get a full measure of value for the money you spend.

While it's easy enough to say, "Buy from a reputable jeweler," many persons do not have access to one. Be that as it may, when purchasing an item of relatively high value, it is wise to have some knowledge of what you are buying. There are those who want to know why a 1-carat diamond may be purchased for $100 and another of the same weight for $5000 or more. For some of the reasons, read on.

The first step in learning about diamonds is to examine some. Go to several stores where diamonds may be purchased and ask to see stones of various sizes and quality. You will be amazed at the differences told you.

Diamonds, unlike automobiles or watches, have no

"suggested" retail price set by manufacturers. There are no universally accepted standards of grading for quality and color. Because of this, the buyer must beware when doing business with unknown dealers. There are jewelers who conform to exacting standards, but those standards may vary from those of other jewelers. It's quite confusing. However, stores with high standards in diamond evaluation are extremely few, compared to the many selling this commodity. An official of one of the largest department stores in the nation stated recently that "a diamond is the single blindest object a person can buy." He added that federal action may be necessary to set up standards.

I included a few chapters on how best to buy a diamond in my book *Fascination of Diamonds* and was surprised at the hundreds of grateful messages from readers who had benefited. One, written from England, stated in part, "As an American living temporarily in Bristol, I came across your book at the local library here. It has given me great pleasure, and it saved me from purchasing an inferior diamond ring of 1.50 carats. For this I must thank you."

Let us try to remove the bandages from the eyes of our "blind" object and learn a little of the qualities which determine a diamond's value. The following chapters will not make you an expert, but at least you will be able to shop with somewhat more confidence.

When diamonds leave the mines, they are divided into hundreds of classifications based on shape, color, and size. The cutters then shape the individual gems, giving each its fire and luster. This skill plays a large part in establishing the ultimate price of the stone, for the price varies according to quality. Nothing can be done about the quality that nature gave a stone, but skillful cutting will bring out its assets to the greatest advantage.

While it has been stated that no two diamonds, like fingerprints, are identical, they may be classified so that a realistic understanding is possible.

Four factors are involved in determining the value of the diamond. They are sometimes referred to as the four C's, and three of them, *color, clarity,* and *cut,* relate to quality. The fourth, *carat,* refers to the weight, and obviously the size of the stone is an important consideration.

With the increase in excellent imitation diamonds, a question asked often is how one can identify a real diamond.

This is relatively easy for a jeweler. He has the experience and the instruments to back up his judgment. But for the layman, it is difficult. There are no simple rules which can be used by the layman as a yardstick. An experienced jeweler usually can tell by simply looking at a diamond, the way a bank teller can tell genuine banknotes from counterfeits. But, as we know, on occasion even bank tellers are fooled.

When a jeweler is in doubt, he can use an instrument called a refractometer, which measures the way light rays are bent as they pass through the stone. The diamond, of course, bends light waves in a characteristic manner. Or the jeweler may use a spectroscope, which measures the various colors of light passing through a stone. Here again, the diamond has certain identifiable characteristics. Other instruments measure the specific gravity of a stone, or subject it to high magnification so that its internal structure can be studied.

A crude way of determining whether a stone is a genuine diamond is the hardness test. Since the diamond is the hardest mineral, it can scratch any other gem. But this test has definite dangers. If the tested stone is indeed another diamond, there is the possibility of injuring either or both stones.

Of course, no reputable firm would dare misrepresent an imitation as a genuine diamond. But be warned against buying a "bargain" from a stranger or unknown source. Even if the stone is in a beautiful platinum setting, there is no assurance that the center is the real article, as gullible buyers have learned to their sorrow.

Now, let us examine each of the four C's in detail.

2

The Meaning of "Carat"

Carat is a unit of weight. It is involved in the price of a diamond at every stage—from the mine to the ultimate consumer.

In olden times, gem merchants used seeds of the carob, a Mediterranean evergreen, whence comes the word carat, in weighing stones. These seeds are remarkably uniform in weight. I've weighed a quantity; they are not precise, weighing from .81 to 1.15 carats. But the average came mighty close to the standard carat in use today.

As systems of weights improved, the seeds were replaced by more scientific measurements. It became common practice to weigh gems in milligrams. There were international disputes, though, as late as 1850, because some jewelers (Belgium) used 188 milligrams to the carat, while others (Italy) as high as 215. The French were prime movers in resolving the confusion. They advocated a carat of 205 milligrams. This finally was modified to 200 milligrams by the International Congress of Weights and Measures, and in 1913 the United States became a party to the agreement. This metric carat, 200 milligrams or 1/142 ounce avoirdupois, is divided into 100 parts, called points. It is the only one of the four C's which is standard worldwide.

When I first entered the jewelry business, I occasionally came across a diamond whose carat had been divided into 64 parts; 1 carat was 64/64 and half a carat 32/64. Other weights were indicated as 33/64, 27/64, etc. I was glad to see the metric carat fully used, for now we had the diamond, like our dollar, divided into 100 parts, with each point compared to each

Carob seeds, which are remarkably uniform in weight—the basis of the carat.
Credit: Jewelers Circular-Keystone

cent. Thus, a stone weighing 1 carat is 100 points (1.00 carat). A half-carat stone weighs 50 points (.50 carat). A diamond weighing 1½ carats is indicated 1.50 carat.

Few stones weigh exactly 1 carat, or 1½ carat. More often they will be .96 carat, 1.02 carat, .47 carat, .51 carat, or whatever. Each point represents money, so if a stone is advertised as "about 1½ carat," or "approximately 1 carat," you would be well advised to ascertain the exact weight. A diamond advertised as "about 1 carat" may be somewhat smaller and be worth considerably less than a 1-carat stone.

The larger the diamond, the scarcer and the more costly *per carat*. In diamond mining, about ten tons of rock can be expected to produce several diamonds whose combined weight would add up to about 1 carat. But to find a rough stone large enough to produce a single finished 1-carat stone, approximately 250 tons of material are processed!

It stands to reason, then, that a 1-carat stone is worth more than two stones weighing a half-carat each, provided,

Diameters and Corresponding Weights of
Round, Ideally Proportioned, Brilliant-Cut Diamonds

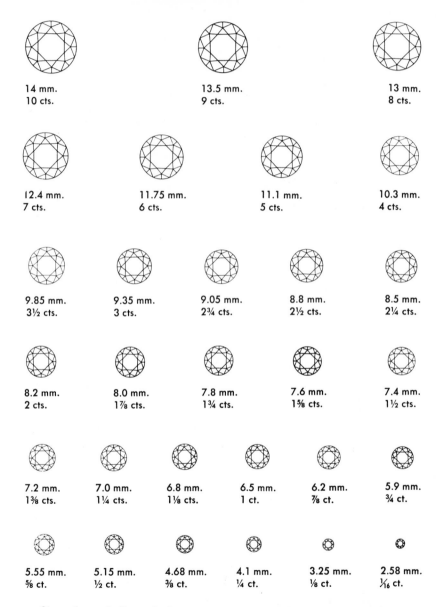

14 mm.
10 cts.

13.5 mm.
9 cts.

13 mm.
8 cts.

12.4 mm.
7 cts.

11.75 mm.
6 cts.

11.1 mm.
5 cts.

10.3 mm.
4 cts.

9.85 mm.
3½ cts.

9.35 mm.
3 cts.

9.05 mm.
2¾ cts.

8.8 mm.
2½ cts.

8.5 mm.
2¼ cts.

8.2 mm.
2 cts.

8.0 mm.
1⅞ cts.

7.8 mm.
1¾ cts.

7.6 mm.
1⅝ cts.

7.4 mm.
1½ cts.

7.2 mm.
1⅜ cts.

7.0 mm.
1¼ cts.

6.8 mm.
1⅛ cts.

6.5 mm.
1 ct.

6.2 mm.
⅞ ct.

5.9 mm.
¾ ct.

5.55 mm.
⅝ ct.

5.15 mm.
½ ct.

4.68 mm.
⅜ ct.

4.1 mm.
¼ ct.

3.25 mm.
⅛ ct.

2.58 mm.
1⁄16 ct.

Sizes of round diamonds from 1/16 carat to 10 carats. Credit: Gemological Institute of America

of course, that the other three C's are equal. As an example, if a half-carat diamond is worth $900, a stone of similar quality in 1-carat size is worth $2800.

When purchasing a diamond ring, it is important to determine the exact size of the center, or principal stone, because that is where the greatest value lies. If the ring is described as "1 carat total weight," that would include several smaller stones used to embellish the setting, and you would not be buying a 1-carat diamond. In searching for an example while writing this chapter, I picked up a newspaper at random and found an advertisement for a cluster ring which promised in large letters: "Our 3-carat diamond is on sale for only X dollars." Then in much smaller type was the explanation that it took a total of twenty-one diamonds to add up to three carats.

Many dealers make it a practice to note the exact weight of the stone on the sales slip. If this isn't done, you would be wise to request it. The information is good protection for reasons such as identification and insurance. Loose diamonds are weighed on very accurate scales. Mounted stones also can be measured by instruments to a remarkable degree of accuracy.

An interesting observation is that a well-cut and proportioned 1-carat diamond is almost exactly one-fourth inch in diameter.

To conclude the lesson on weight, if a ring is described to you as "our Empress Model for $250," be sure to ask the weight of the Empress, particularly the weight of the center stone.

3
How Clarity Affects Value

Every diamond is graded for clarity, which has to do with the internal quality of the stone, meaning imperfections (or inclusions) and blemishes of any kind. Few diamonds are entirely free of them. In stones over ½ carat, ninety-nine percent will have some internal imperfection.

Flaws may vary from a tiny white spot very difficult to see even under ten-power magnification, accepted as the international standard, to large and numerous blemishes. These spots may be transparent or opaque. All lower the value of the diamond. An infinitesimal white spot affects the value least. The larger and more numerous the inclusions, the more they downgrade the stone's value.

Don't be alarmed if told that the diamond is not flawless. By far, most stones being worn today are not. It is just that flaws are a dominant factor in the gem's worth.

It is your privilege to examine a diamond the same way the jeweler does—under his ten-power magnifier, called a loupe. Don't be afraid to ask for it. It might take several minutes to get used to it, but once you have the stone in focus, you are on your way to learning a bit about diamonds. Any jeweler of repute will gladly assist you to see what inclusions are present. The color and cut of the stone can be fairly well judged by the naked eye when you learn what to look for, but you will need help to locate flaws that affect clarity.

The position of the inclusions also makes a difference. A spot in the center of the table (the flat octagonal facet at the top of a round diamond) would impair the value more than if it were on the edge, or in the lower half.

There are many types of imperfections, each with a specific name:

Carbon spots—These are by far the most numerous. Although they appear black to the eye, they are not really carbon spots. But that is what they're called. They may be just a tiny speck, or they may be large and numerous.

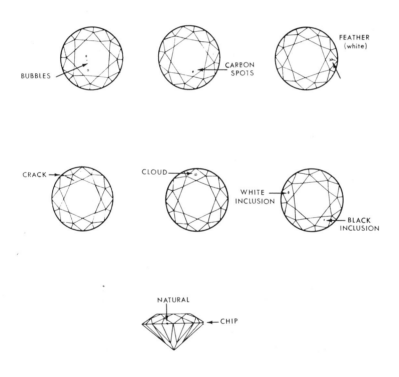

Seven illustrations showing how defects affect the value of diamonds.

Bubble—Transparent, roundish inclusions of any size. These are actually small imbedded crystals, or grains of a different material within the host crystal.

Cloud—A group of white transparent spots which, if in sufficient quantity, can give that part of the stone a slightly clouded appearance.

Feather—A cleavage or fracture which occasionally takes on the appearance of a feather, although other shapes may be included in this category. Some jewelers call all transparent inclusions of odd shapes "feathers."

Cleavage crack—A crack in the stone along a line of cleavage (the grain of the stone). Such a flaw may affect the durability of the diamond. This brings up a point worth repeating. A diamond has cleavage directions, like a piece of wood. If struck against a hard object along a cleavage direction, the diamond may be chipped or damaged. Remember that a diamond is a precious object. It always should be handled with care and respect.

Chip—A small curved break on a stone, extending from its edge.

Natural—A pit or blemish on the outer edge (girdle) of the diamond. It may be part of the original surface of the rough stone left by the cutter to avoid weight loss. If tiny and contained within the width of the girdle, most competent graders do not classify it as an imperfection. However, sometimes a natural is quite obvious and goes beyond the boundary of the girdle.

Nick—A tiny chip out of the stone's surface, usually found on the girdle.

Extra facet—A facet in excess of the number needed for maximum brilliance. They usually are used to cover a chip, nick, or other blemish on the surface. Some graders do not regard extra facets as blemishes if they can't be seen through the crown (upper part) or if they are not on the crown itself. Other graders definitely regard them as imperfections. Avoid an extra facet if you wish a "flawless" diamond. Otherwise, it is not a bad fault.

Bearded girdle—Numerous hair-like fractures extending within the girdle. These are caused by faulty rounding by the cutter, which leaves the girdle with a fuzzy appearance instead of being smooth.

Are there diamonds without any of these imperfections? Yes, but they are rare and are among the costliest. The Federal Trade Commission has ruled that no diamond may be classified as flawless if it discloses any flaw, crack, spots, white or black blemishes, or imperfections of any kind when examined loose, by a competent observer using ten-power magnification. Few gems can pass such a test. Flawless is not the same as "perfect," which I will explain later.

The general brilliance and beauty of diamonds are not affected by inclusions unless they are large enough to be seen by the naked eye. Cut and color have much more to do with a stone's beauty than minor inclusions. However, keep in mind that, even though inclusions do not mar the appearance of a stone, the tiniest imperfections lower its value.

There is no standard system of classifying diamonds according to the extent of their imperfections. Some jewelers designate a flawless stone as zero. A stone with a very minute inclusion would be classified 1, a slightly less perfect gem would be 2, and so on. Another jeweler might use letters A, B, and C. Many use the terms VVSI (very, very slight inclusion, or very, very slight imperfection); VSI (very slight inclusion); SI (slight inclusion or imperfection); and Imperfect, which would cover a wide range of flaws. These private classification codes are quite arbitrary and do not mean a great deal provided you ask about the flaws and the jeweler points them out to you.

It is to your advantage to examine stones loose, before they are set. A tiny inclusion which may be seen when the stone is loose might not be visible when it is set. Many jewelers show diamonds loose. However, the average jeweler can't afford to carry a large stock of both loose and mounted stones.

What diamond dealers tell you about their stones may be startlingly different, but after you have looked at a few diamonds with a ten-power eye loupe you can start forming opinions of your own. A misleading term used occasionally is "eye perfect." The connotation is of fine quality, but its real meaning is that the stone is flawed but not to the extent that the inclusions can be seen by the naked eye. The best jewelers frown on this term. Diamonds should never be graded without using the ten-power magnifier. Another ambiguous term is "ninety percent or ninety-five percent perfect." This is meaningless, as the jeweler can apply any percentage he chooses.

Another meaningless term is "Our very finest quality," used in some diamond catalogs. The chances are their "very finest" may be nowhere near as fine as the finest quality carried in your retail jeweler's regular stock. All such terms are relative, and the only real test is in careful, personal inspection. It is to your advantage to use every possible aid in examining a stone. If your jeweler has special equipment, such as a binocular microscope, ask him to use it to show you inclusions. A reputable dealer should be proud to give you a demonstration of his specialized equipment.

To summarize, the best diamond to buy is a stone with as few and as small inclusions as possible, consistent with what you wish to spend. Avoid those with noticeable cracks, as they are most likely to be damaged; also avoid those with spots visible to the naked eye. You may have to settle for a smaller diamond, but for true enjoyment, size should be secondary to beauty.

Above all, don't hesitate about asking questions when shopping. After all, you don't buy diamonds every day and you are entitled to find out all you can before making a purchase. If a jeweler is reluctant to answer your questions clearly, try someone else.

4

What Cut Does for the Diamond

Of the four C's, carat, color, cut, and clarity, only the cutting involves the human factor.

Even if a diamond is flawless internally and its color the best, only skillful cutting can bring out its maximum beauty. In this art, precision is the key. Every facet of the stone must be symmetrical and the angles must be arrived at with the utmost accuracy.

A skilled cutter improves nature's rough stone by precise cutting and shaping to give it the brilliant fire which makes it the most prized of all gems. A skilled cutter can bring out every possible bit of the beauty which nature built into the stone. A less skilled cutter, given the same stone, might fail to develop it to its full potential.

Cut has two meanings. One, the verb, means the sawing, faceting, proportioning, and polishing, which will be discussed later in this section. The other meaning, the noun, refers to the shape into which the stone is fashioned.

The most popular shapes are shown in the illustration which follows. Others, used as embellishments in settings, are shown elsewhere.

No. 1 is called the emerald cut. It is distinguished by its flat face or table.
No. 2 is the round or brilliant cut.
No. 3 is the oval.
No. 4, the pear shape, occasionally is called pendeloque.

No. 5, the marquise, pronounced mar-KEYS, is also called boat-shaped.

No. 6 is heart-shaped.

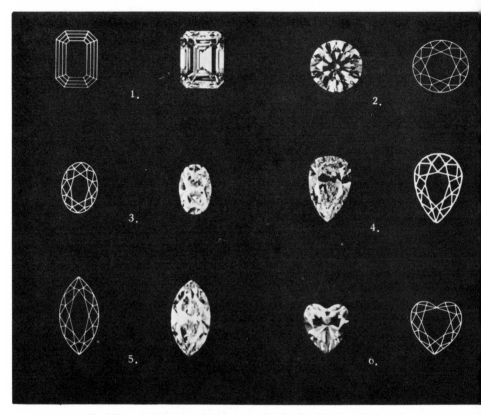

Six different styles of cut diamonds. Credit: N. W. Ayer & Son, Inc.

The shape into which the diamond is cut depends primarily on its shape in the rough. While a diamond is cut to bring out its beauty and brilliance, it must be remembered that, in the process, flaws must be eliminated. At the same time, the loss in weight and size must be kept to a minimum.

The loss in cutting and fashioning a diamond is tremendous. In some shapes, the loss can exceed seventy percent. In round shapes, fully half of the rough can be lost in creating a stone of excellent proportions.

Since the round- or "brilliant"- cut diamond is the best known, the comments which follow will apply primarily to that shape. To understand the "why" of cutting, it is necessary to know that a diamond is a light trap and light concentrator. The stone must be cut so that the rays of light, striking the various facets and entering the stone, are reflected out through the top in highly concentrated form. The more light focused up through the top, the more brilliant the stone will be.

Cutting has another function. It brings out the diamond's power of light dispersion—its ability to separate the white light entering the stone into the many colors of the spectrum. A well-cut diamond sends back to your eye a dazzling array of brilliant hues.

To cut a round diamond of about 1 carat, it usually takes a day for the sawing. The rounding requires half an hour. Another six to eight hours go into the final faceting and polishing. All this is assuming there are no problems and all goes smoothly. Some shapes take longer; a marquise can take from three to five days to attain its ultimate form.

At this point, it might be well to become reacquainted with some of the terms used in the diamond-cutting trade:

The table—The stone's largest facet at the top; in round diamonds the table is an octagon.
Facet—One of the flat surfaces or planes of the stone.
Crown—The upper part of the stone above the girdle.
Girdle—The extreme outside edge of the diamond.
Pavilion—The lower part; that under the girdle.
Culet—The very bottom facet. Ideally, it should be very small and closed.
Make—This refers to the correctness of proportions, the finishing and polishing, and the symmetry of the stone.
Finish—The excellence of the polish, the smoothness of the girdle, and the tininess of the culet.

Full cut is the term for a diamond which has been

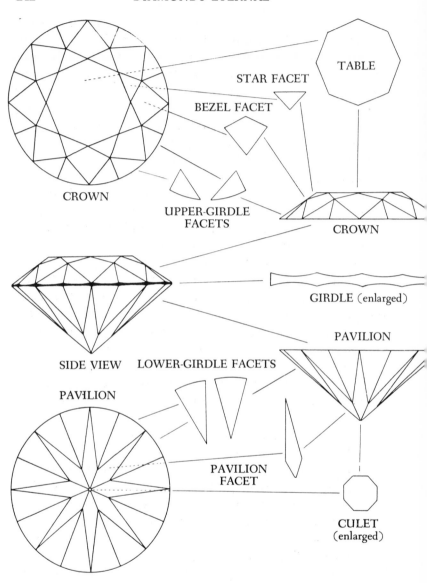

Girdle—the extreme outside edge of the stone. Crown—that part of the stone above the girdle. Credit: Gemological Institute of America

given fifty-eight facets. There are thirty-two facets above the girdle, plus the table for a total of thirty-three. Below the girdle, the pavilion has twenty-four facets, plus the culet. Thus, the total is fifty-eight facets. Each of the facets must be properly placed, sized, and angled to achieve the greatest brilliance.

Very small diamonds used in settings and jewelry—in the one-, two-, and three- point range—are generally cut with only seventeen facets. They have eight above the

BRILLIANT CUT

58 facets. Cut exactly the same whether diamond is large or small (except for omission of tiny facet at point in very small stones).

SINGLE CUT

17 facets. Found in very small stones used for decoration, as on the shoulders of a ring, etc.

MARQUISE

58 facets. Proportion of width to length varies slightly according to shape of rough.

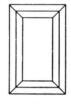

BAGUETTE

25 facets. Baguette means "little stick." Used for decoration and in elaborate designs.

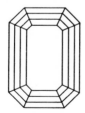

EMERALD CUT

58 facets. Rectangular shape with facets polished along the sides and diagonally across the corners.

SQUARE CUT

30 facets. Used most often in working out designs for jewelry.

Single cut and baguette diamonds. Credit: Gemological Institute of America

girdle and eight below, plus the table. The culet is not used. These are called "single cut." When diamonds of the smallest size—one point or less—are fully cut with fifty-eight facets, they often take on a slightly fuzzy look. Stones of three points or larger should be full cut for maximum brilliance.

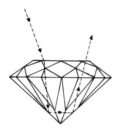 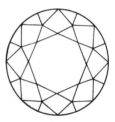

Study the sketch. Notice how the light enters a properly cut diamond, is reflected from facet to facet, and comes back through the top of the stone in a brilliant rainbow blaze.

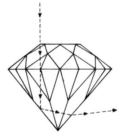 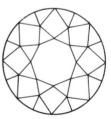

In a stone that is disproportionately deep, much of the light is reflected to opposite facets at the wrong angle for returning through the top of the diamond and is lost through the sides.

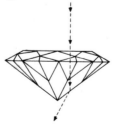 

Three styles of cutting. Credit: Gemological Institute of America

In a shallow stone, much of the light fails to be reflected and "leaks" out at the bottom. These are sometimes called swindled stones made to look as large as possible.

In order to obtain the maximum brilliancy as shown in the sketch, certain formulas have been developed. The American cut, also called the Ideal cut, calls for the table to be approximately fifty-three percent of the diameter of the diamond. The crown should be about one-fourth of the depth of the stone, and the lower part about three-fourths. The total depth should be sixty percent of the diameter. The girdle should be very thin—one to two percent of the stone's depth.

The European cut differs slightly from the American cut. It has a slightly larger diameter of the table and a slightly higher crown, with the pavilion slightly lower. The depth including the girdle equals fifty-nine percent of the diameter. The angles differ slightly.

In order to achieve its highest potential, any style of cutting—emerald cut, pear shape, oval, marquise, or whatever—must adhere to strict standards, just as in the round. For example, if the table of an emerald-cut diamond is very large, taking almost the entire top of the

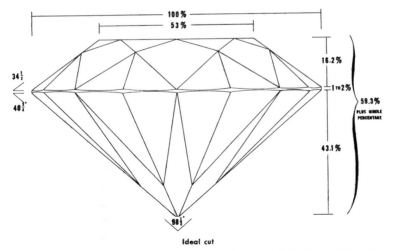

Ideal cut

The Ideal- or American-cut diamond. Credit: Gemological Institute of America

stone, as it frequently does, the value is lessened for a good reason. The diamond is still beautiful, but it would have more brilliancy if the crown weren't so flat. Approximately a fourth of the stone should be above the girdle and three-fourths below to achieve an ideally proportioned gem.

Very few diamonds are cut to the most ideal standards because a maximum loss of weight would be incurred. However, if the cut doesn't vary too much from the ideal, the stone can still be very attractive and will be in a reasonable price range.

What is the best shape to buy? This is entirely a matter of personal choice. The round has always been the traditional and most popular. In the larger sizes, 3 to 5 carats and over, some prefer the emerald, pear, marquise, or oval. The round, when properly cut, is the most brilliant. With many persons, the beauty in appearance of

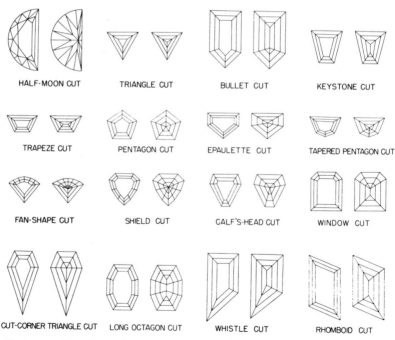

Various styles of cut diamonds for ring mountings and jewelry. Credit: Gemological Institute of America

the other shapes more than makes up for the lesser brilliance.

It takes many years to train a diamond cutter and, just as some surgeons are more skillful than others, some cutters are more competent than others. Most cutting factories insist that their workers cut the diamonds to bring out the best in the stones. Inevitably, however, there are a few that specialize in cutting stones to return the greatest possible weight, and this means stones of inferior cut, lacking in brilliancy and fire.

In stones with shallow cut, and with very thin girdles, there not only is a loss of brilliancy, but there also is an extra hazard of damage to the girdle after the diamond has been worn for a comparatively short time.

When a cutter lacks skill, or integrity, he may turn out a stone whose girdle is too thick, or wavy, or not parallel to the table. Occasionally a brilliant-cut diamond is noticeably out of round, or it has a bearded girdle and extra facets, which I described in the section on clarity. These are flaws to be looked for in examining the stone under the jeweler's loupe.

The term "perfect cut," which you may come across, is a misleading one. A perfectly cut stone is very seldom encountered; they are far rarer than flawless stones, which are plentiful by comparison. Exercise caution when you hear this term.

If you are told that the diamond is perfectly cut because it has fifty-eight facets, the salesman is either ignorant or trying to misrepresent his merchandise. As I've pointed out, fifty-eight facets is the standard.

If you are told that a particular 2-carat stone looks like a 3-carat one, that would be the very reason why you shouldn't buy that one. A 2-carat stone of good proportions should look like a 2-carat stone. If it doesn't, it is out of proportion.

Most diamonds found in reliable establishments are well cut. The ones to watch out for are those that deviate so much from the standard that beauty is sacrificed. As a rule, if diamonds of the same size vary appreciably in brilliance, chances are the difference is due to the cutting.

By looking at many stones, you will be able to see what makes one diamond superior to another in the very important C called the cut. A beautifully cut diamond is a fine example of how man's knowledge and skill have been applied to one of nature's wonderful creations to achieve infinite beauty.

5

Color and Its Importance

The finest and most expensive diamonds are totally without color, like a drop of distilled water. The rainbow hues it flashes derive from the light it separates into the colors of the spectrum.

There is one exception to the above statement. A few diamonds are found with natural tints of pink, green, blue, canary, and other hues. Because such stones are so rare, they are cherished and very expensive.

However, practically all diamonds classified as white have varying degrees of yellow or brown tint, and very, very few fall into the category described at the start of this chapter.

Given two diamonds of equal weight and clarity, would the color or cut be the more important factor in establishing its value? Many jewelers think cutting is, because good cutting is most essential to a diamond's beauty. Others, and I am in this category, contend color is the more important. Certainly it has more bearing on the diamond's value, for a poorly cut stone, if it is large enough, can be recut. But there is nothing that can be done about faulty color. Let's compare two diamonds each weighing a carat, each well cut and proportioned, and each flawless. A difference in color might result in one stone being worth many hundred dollars more than the other.

Let me stress that a diamond with enough yellow to be readily apparent to the untrained eye still can be a brilliant and beautiful stone. Nonetheless, the rule is that the greater the degree of yellow, the less its value.

Some jewelers use an instrument which electronically establishes the amount of yellow a diamond transmits. Others use a different instrument, whereby the diamond to be tested is placed under a white light which is constant and free of ultraviolet rays and compared to a set of master stones whose colors have been accurately graded. There are other ways, but the majority of diamond sellers do not have these aids. As a result, the very important C of color is a comparatively unknown factor.

So far, there is no universally accepted standard for measuring color. Members of the American Gem Society use numerals from 0 to 10, zero being colorless. The Gemological Institute of America uses letters, D standing for colorless, on to P for light yellow, then on to X for the

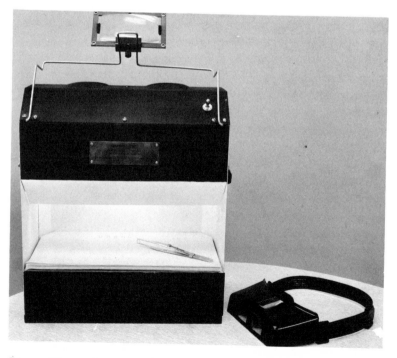

Diamondlite—an instrument for color grading, for visual comparison of master diamonds. Credit: Gemological Institute of America

real yellows. The Europeans use terms which may still be encountered in the United States, like River, Top Wesselton, Wesselton, Top Crystal, Crystal, etc. The United Kingdom starts with Finest White, Fine White, Commercial White, and on down the line.

But, as in cut and clarity, there is no accepted standard used by all. The majority of jewelers follow no standard except their own and some ignore the color factor entirely. Naturally, this has led to unfortunate and misleading terms applied to grades of color.

Who has not heard the term "blue-white"? In England, the term is sometimes used as an alternative to their Finest White, their very top color. But in the United States, blue-white has been so misused that no ethical jeweler uses it. I remember stores which used to advertise themselves as "The Home of Blue-White Diamonds." It is doubtful that they knew what the term meant. Extremely few diamonds have any blue body color in them and, therefore, the term is useless in describing a diamond. If a jeweler insists on using it, you had better shop elsewhere.

Another term to avoid in the United States is Commercial White. In Great Britain, this term implies fine white color, but it has been so abused here that it is avoided by ethical jewelers.

Our Federal Trade Commission has ruled that color should be graded when the diamond is viewed in normal, north daylight. However, north light can vary by season, hour, day to day, and even latitude. (Since direct sunlight with its rays of varying length flatters a diamond, it is impossible to determine body color under it.)

If your jeweler lacks a color-grading instrument, or doesn't use an understandable system, look at the stone in north light (in the Northern Hemisphere) on a cloudless day. Always examine the diamond from the side; any yellow content is more noticeable this way than when you look straight down into the stone. Only when diamonds are unmounted may their true color be accurately judged. A few jewelers show them this way, but the average jeweler just couldn't afford both a loose and mounted stock of diamonds, as mentioned before, even if he wished to show them loose.

A good trick is to breathe on a diamond. This sometimes tends to bring out a yellow tint that otherwise wouldn't show up, and it is a good trick to remember in the absence of more scientific instruments.

Since diamonds reflect the color of their surroundings, don't look at a stone under a jeweler's blue lamp. It will look quite different in a different light. On the other hand, a diamond doesn't show its best under fluorescent lights or when the light is poor.

Color, more than a diamond's other attributes, affects value so much that again, if at all possible, buy from a reputable merchant who can explain the fine points of this quality to your satisfaction.

6

Some Important Questions and Answers about Diamonds

The foregoing chapters covered a lot of ground, so let us do some summarizing in question and answer form.

How Should I Buy a Diamond?

Having read what you have on the subject, your best bet still is to go to a reliable dealer. This is your surest protection. If you don't know of a store where you buy without question, shop around. Prices vary even in reliable stores due to high overhead expense and other factors. Shopping for a diamond can be fun. Don't hurry. With the knowledge you have acquired on the subject, the stone you select after careful study will have more meaning for you.

What Is the Best Diamond to Buy?

The one which is best for you, and that depends on how much you can spend.

For those who can afford the best, remember clarity, cut, and color. The stone must be flawless. The cut, proportions, and finish must be exact and the color with no trace of yellow or brown. A stone with all these characteristics will be the most expensive, but ownership of such a gem will give you the pride of possessing the best specimen of nature's greatest jewel.

Most persons will settle for something less and still find great enjoyment in the diamond. Pick a stone of good

253

cut and color, having only minor inclusions, and—for the same amount you would pay for the finest—you will be able to purchase a somewhat larger diamond. Keep in mind that very small inclusions will affect the beauty of a stone less than inferior cut and color. Buy the best stone you can afford.

What Should I Look for in Choosing My Diamond?

In brief, look for beauty, brilliance, and fire. Scintillation, or the twinkle of the stone when it is moved about, is important. While only an expert can evaluate the placing of the facets and angles, any major shortcomings will become apparent to you if a stone is compared to others. In other words, examine several stones at the same time. Look at the stone from all sides. Is the girdle on a straight line and parallel to the table? Are the table and culet lined up properly?

Look at the stone from the top. Is the table disproportionately large? If it is, some of your friends might think it a large stone, but its real value would be open to question. Look at two or more stones of the same size and you may detect a slight difference in brilliance. This would be due in great part to cutting. Take the one which looks best to you.

You've said so many times, "Go to a reputable jeweler." But what if I'm not quite certain about the jeweler I'm doing business with?

There are no merchants more ethical than those who deal in diamonds. At the same time, there are no greater misrepresentations than those offered by unethical dealers who take advantage of the public's lack of knowledge about diamonds. If you aren't sure about the merchandise you are being shown, look around. Make comparisons.

Chances are, after reading this book thoroughly, you will know more about diamonds than the untrained salesman who characterizes stores where ethical standards are less than the highest. If the salesclerk is vague, or he gives you answers that contradict what you've learned here, it's time to do your diamond shopping elsewhere.

I have a friend who has access to a "wholesale" catalog. How about this?

Some catalogs of this sort, available to business houses, banks, individuals, etc., have good prices on many items. But the diamonds should be scrutinized carefully. The prices listed as "wholesale" are usually no lower, and often higher, than the retail prices of legitimate dealers. The "retail" prices listed in most of these catalogs are almost always inflated. Frequently, they misrepresent on color and clarity grades, and you have no way of examining a diamond you buy through a catalog.

I purchased a mail-order diamond described as AAAAA color, finest cut, finest quality, so that I could evaluate it. I wasn't surprised to see its qualities were far short of what they wanted to convey. There are few bargains in diamonds. Compare values and see for yourself.

Could I get a good deal from a private party?

You might, if you are buying from a trusted friend who is willing to sacrifice his diamond for quick money. But both of you would be wise to have the stone appraised by a competent jeweler. The appraisal fee will be well spent and you will still be friends, even if you don't buy it. But beware of diamonds offered for sale in the want-ad columns. The bargain could be most legitimate. On the other hand, there are individuals who make a good living by buying diamonds from jewelers and reselling them to gullible individuals at a fat profit under the guise of distress selling.

I see diamonds advertised frequently by large, well-known department stores at special bargain prices. What do you say to that?

Let me reiterate: There are few bargains in diamonds. There's a sale on diamonds going on all the time in any large city. Some time ago I asked the chairman of the board of one of our large department stores some pointed questions about their "special diamond values." He admitted the store leased out the diamond department and he didn't know anything about the operation. It is amazing how a good store is willing to lend its name to situations like this, but it all comes under the heading of business, I suppose.

High-pressure sales tactics are designed to take advantage of the average person's unfamiliarity with diamonds. Years ago a New York department store advertised "flawless, fine quality" diamonds for figures well under the going rate. Examination of the stones revealed them as imperfect, poor-quality specimens.

In a court suit which followed, the manager of the store explained, "It is simply a difference of opinion between experts in a highly technical business." Perhaps so, but you don't want to be caught on the short end of such a difference of opinion. Don't be greedy; if you expect to find an unusual buy, it could turn out to be very costly.

Do "guaranteed" diamonds protect you?

A guarantee is only as good as the firm who issues it. I have in my souvenirs a "Diamond Guarantee Bond" issued by a cut-rate jewelry firm. Sold for $350, a half-carat stone was described as "AA" quality, whatever that means. The stone had important imperfections, with an approximate retail value at the time of $275. I am sure that if the owner of the stone had taken it back, along with the guarantee, he could have had it exchanged for another overpriced, inferior stone. What good is such a guarantee?

How about loan firms and liquidation sales?

Some are legitimate, like anything else. But in many instances, if the diamonds were as represented, the firms advertising wouldn't have to go to the expense of putting on a sale. Retail jewelers would snap them up.

You mentioned a "perfect" diamond. Is there any such thing?

The Federal Trade Commission states that a stone classified as "perfect" must be flawless, of good cut and proportions, and of excellent color when examined by a qualified grader using ten-power magnification. These terms can vary in meaning to many "qualified" graders. What one will call excellent color may be graded notches below by another. The same applies to cut. Only when told by a store of unquestioned integrity that a diamond is "perfect" should you place entire faith in the term. Yes, there are "perfect" stones, but they are rare.*

Should I always have a diamond appraised before a purchase?

Not if you know your seller. But appraisal is a good idea when you are doing business with strangers or when a cut-rate dealer urges you to do so to make sure of a "tremendous value." There are unethical appraisers, just as there are unethical jewelers. It is not unusual for such sellers to send you for an inflated evaluation to an appraiser with whom they have an understanding. Pick your own.

Aren't you making the purchase of a diamond seem a very risky adventure?

An adventure it certainly is, whether you are buying a diamond for your own enjoyment, an engagement ring, a stone for a loving wife who has been your helpmate on the road to success, or a large gem as a long-term investment. But it need not be a risky adventure if you heed the things I have explained in this book.

And finally, when considering a purchase, take your time. Compare. Ask questions. Look around. And enjoy your experience. You will buy many things in life whose

* Again, it must be remembered that "flawless" means no imperfections in the diamond, as described in the chapter on clarity. "Perfect" means not only that, but the cut must be in excellent proportions, and the color must be in the Best classification.

cost far exceeds what you spend for a diamond, but none will provide quite the same thrilling and lasting pleasure. A diamond is forever. You should never be hasty in making such an important investment in happiness.

7

Diamonds as an Investment

Jewelers are asked almost every day whether diamonds are a good investment. There is no simple answer. The reply has to be: "It depends."

Even though diamonds and investments are synonymous in the minds of some persons, many discover that it is impossible to sell their gems at a price even close to the original cost.

This is especially true in the low-price ranges, where there is no scarcity of goods and where the retailer's profit margin is greater. While it is customary for a jeweler to take back a diamond at full value if you purchased a more expensive stone, he will be reluctant to buy it for cash at the price you paid for it. And why should he? The jeweler, like any other merchant, must make a profit on the sale if he is to remain in business. Moreover, he has plenty of other diamonds in his stock which must be sold, so he probably would not pay you his own cost on the item. So then you take the diamond to another dealer who makes an offer you consider disappointing, and you start to think you were cheated.

The fact is that you can't buy a diamond, or any other commodity, at retail and expect to sell it for the same price to a dealer who buys at wholesale.

No, the kind of diamond most of us can afford—low-and medium-priced ones—shouldn't be considered an investment at all. I have been asked scores of times about the investment potential of a $200 ring at the time it was being purchased for entirely different

259

reasons, and my answer always was: "Enjoy the diamond; don't consider it as an investment."

The best that can be said for a low- and medium-priced diamond is that, long after a much costlier fur coat or automobile have been discarded as worthless, the diamond has some value and will bring something, even if not anything like the original cost. This is, in itself, no small consideration.

The other side of the investment story is that fine large diamonds have appreciated over the years. In the 1960s, dealers from foreign countries swarmed into New York and bought quantities of the finest available stones, thus starting the movement. The interest of French, German, Italian, Swiss, and other foreign dealers who descended on this country's wholesale headquarters was linked to the large gold outflow at the time. No doubt they anticipated an eventual devaluation of the dollar, possibly their booming economy was a consideration, and, finally, they wanted a hedge in case their own currencies were devalued.

Europeans are much more realistic about diamonds than Americans. Many of the well-to-do try to keep at least twenty-five percent of their resources in precious gems as a hedge against unstable currencies and because they are an easily portable asset readily convertible into cash in emergencies.

Just before World War II, thousands of persons were able to flee Hitler's Germany because their diamonds supplied the means to pay bribes and buy passage. More recently, wealthy Cubans used diamonds to flee their country.

A few years ago, when the Japan Philharmonic Orchestra played in my home city of Denver, several of the musicians came into our store to buy diamonds. The Japanese are developing into a solid diamond-purchasing nation, buying them for investment as well as pleasure and accounting for an incredible twenty percent of the world's consumption of cut stones. Such buying pressures add significantly to recent price appreciation.

The prices of diamonds were very stable in the 1950s as can be seen in Chart A.

CHART A

	¼ Carat	½ Carat	1 Carat	2 Carats
1949	$90–210	$255–490	$655–1175	$1500–3400
1950	85–205	215–445	520–1090	1200–3120
1951	85–195	220–475	570–1195	1260–3205
1952	85–180	215–425	585–1135	1250–3115
1953	90–195	215–440	570–1180	1280–3190
1954	85–195	200–435	605–1175	1355–3265
1955	85–190	220–450	590–1180	1275–3245
1956	85–215	200–445	540–1170	1295–3300
1957	90–215	210–470	570–1180	1340–3175
1958	95–225	215–485	605–1210	1370–3350
1959	90–220	220–465	560–1240	1540–3455

After 1960, prices started upward, as Chart B shows.

CHART B

	¼ Carat	½ Carat	1 Carat	2 Carats	3 Carats
1960	$75–240	$150–550	$500–1550	$910–4550	$2175– 8650
1961	65–320	160–520	450–1600	1025–4200	1950– 8000
1962	65–320	160–500	450–1500	1200–4500	2400– 8150
1963	60–300	160–590	450–1600	1000–5000	2000– 9000
1964	70–300	175–600	500–1800	1000–5500	3200–12500
1965	70–375	160–800	450–1600	1000–5500	3000–10000
1966	85–375	175–700	600–1850	1250–7000	3000–15000
1967	85–400	175–800	500–2300	1200–8000	3350–16000
1968	75–375	150–800	650–2500	1450–8000	3000–15000
1969	90–400	200–850	600–2500	1500–9000	3500–18000
1970	90–400	200–850	750–2750	2000–9500	3000–20000

The diamonds covered by these prices range from the lower qualities, which vary the most, to the very finest. Medium quality stones would cost about half of the highest price in each class. The prices of the low end stones are misleading because these qualities are somewhat poorer than were sold years ago.

The price of finest quality stones probably will continue to climb. In 1972, the best 1-carat diamonds were being quoted at over $3500, with the larger sizes proportionately higher. If the trend continues, large, gem-quality stones of the finest color will soon be limited to extremely wealthy collectors.

As with other merchandise, diamond prices reflect currency fluctuations. When British currency was devalued some time ago, the prices of diamond rough were raised to compensate for it. When the U.S. dollar was devalued, prices rose to cover the drop. Nonetheless, the diamond syndicate has proved its worth. A disastrous price drop, such as took place when the Brazilian mines opened in 1750, and again when the great South African fields were found in 1869, has not recurred since the formation of the DeBeers Company in 1889.

During the Great Depression of the early 1930s, diamond prices dropped, but this was due in large part to privately owned diamonds being dumped on the market. DeBeers stockpiled its production during this time instead of flooding the market and prevented what could have been a disaster to diamond owners throughout the world. Because of this move, diamonds did much better than other gems.

How would diamond prices react to the emergence of synthetic gem diamonds on the market? I have answered this question in an earlier chapter. In my opinion, they will remain stable because the synthetics can be identified as such. The finest copies of paintings, no matter how good, have never affected the worth of the originals, except possibly to make them even more valuable.

Well, then, should one consider diamonds for investment? If one has abundant stocks and bonds, life

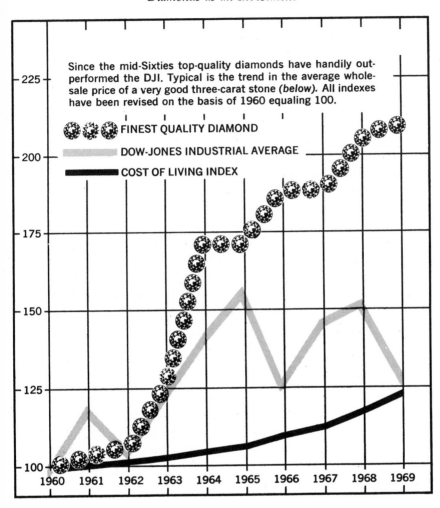

Since the mid-Sixties top-quality diamonds have handily out-performed the DJI. Typical is the trend in the average whole-sale price of a very good three-carat stone *(below).* All indexes have been revised on the basis of 1960 equaling 100.

FINEST QUALITY DIAMOND

DOW-JONES INDUSTRIAL AVERAGE

COST OF LIVING INDEX

Credit: Forbes *Magazine, Investment No. 7*

insurance, and other investments, diamonds could well be a very good next step in diversifying one's holdings. In this country, few are going to need diamonds for a quick getaway. However, with inflation and the continuous erosion of our currency, diamond values should appreciate, and many of the wealthy are investing in them.

It must be remembered, however, that unlike stocks

and bonds, diamonds cannot be turned into cash immediately simply by calling your broker. They can always be sold, but it may take time and effort to find a buyer, just as with objects of art, fine musical instruments, and paintings. Also keep in mind that, in calculating appreciation, you must make up the difference between wholesale and retail prices. If gems must be sold quickly, to settle an estate, for instance, a loss would probably be incurred. The Idol's Eye, a famous diamond formerly owned by a Denverite, brought only half its original cost when the estate was settled. But the man who bought it can afford to hold it indefinitely and is asking a great deal more for it than it originally cost the owner.

The best types of diamonds to buy are those of the finer qualities, regardless of size and shape. To recommend the best sizes is more difficult. If times are good and quick liquidation is likely, the larger sizes would do comparatively well; if times are poor, the small ones would do best.

I would recommend stones between 1 and 3 carats for the average. For those who have no need to fear the liquidation factor and can hold them indefinitely, large sizes should continue to appreciate, as these are presently the scarcest. For investment, loose diamonds are best, as expensive settings get slight consideration at the time of resale. On the other hand, diamonds should be enjoyed, and if they can be worn while being treated as an investment, so much the better.

8

A Word about Insurance

Like anything of value, diamonds should be insured for peace of mind.

The usual Basic Home Owner Policy, as written in most states, currently covers losses up to a maximum of $500 on diamond jewelry. This type of coverage includes theft, burglary, fire, etc.; it excludes mysterious disappearance, loss of diamonds from settings, breakage or chipping of diamonds, and other very possible mishaps.

It is advisable, therefore, to pay an additional premium and obtain a scheduled floater on your diamond jewelry to cover almost everything except wear and tear and inherent vice (basic original defect). Each item to be insured should be listed separately, fully described and valued, and photographed for identification.

There is no point in overinsuring the items as the insurance company reserves the right to replace them "in like kind and quality" rather than paying the full insured value. This is because insurance companies are usually able to buy replacements at a reduced cost. Further, an Actual Cash Value Policy will pay, if replacement is impossible, only the market value of the item lost at time of loss, and less depreciation, and in no event shall exceed the maximum value indicated.

Some insurance companies allow a replacement to be made at the store where your purchase was made. Others will not. If this point is important to you, the time to ask about it is at the time the policy is made out, and not after

265

the loss occurs and when it is in the hands of the company's claim department.

It is well to have your jewelry appraised every year; in fact, many companies are no longer writing three-year term policies, but are having them rewritten every year with up-to-date valuations. A fine large (1 carat or over) diamond which you have had for some time may very well have appreciated in value, so have it reappraised if it hasn't been done recently. Regular appraisals are for your protection, as well as for the insurance company's.

Finally, make sure you understand the terms of your policy. I have seen many misunderstandings which resulted because the insured was not familiar with the contract.

9

Care for Your Diamonds

Diamonds are beautiful gems, but they need a little loving care to keep them so.

Nature went to a lot of trouble to create them; years have been spent in learning how to best cut and polish them so they give maximum beauty and sparkle. Yet they get dirty easily. Why do we see so many diamond rings in need of a little attention? Considering all that went into them to make them what they are, they at least deserve to be kept clean.

I was flattered when Miss Amy Vanderbilt, the famous authority on etiquette, contacted me in regard to diamond care. She had received a letter from a reader and, with Miss Vanderbilt's permission and that of the *Los Angeles Times* Syndicate, I am quoting it and her reply:

Dear Miss Vanderbilt:

I don't happen to have any diamonds to speak of, just my tiny engagement ring. When I look around at my bridge club and see the rocks women wear and how dirty they are, I wonder why you don't talk about the poor manners of dirty diamonds as well as the matter of dirty eyeglasses. Certainly it must be simple enough to clean diamonds at home. What good are they if they don't sparkle? Mine is such a tiny one in a Tiffany setting that I don't really have a problem keeping it clean. Maybe you should tell those women with big diamonds, some of them surrounded by other precious stones, how to give them sparkle. —Mrs. R. G.

A—I agree with you. A diamond wedding band in particular can get soap-embedded, filmed by cosmetics, and women don't seem to notice. I discussed the problem with diamond expert Victor Argenzio. He wrote me as follows:

"I agree entirely with you that it is regrettable that women

267

allow their diamond rings to become dimmed by film and dirt. Diamond rings attract grease, soaps, lotions, creams and so on which come into daily contact with women; and the more frequently diamonds are cleaned, the easier the task.

"In the absence of a prepared diamond cleaner sold at most jewelry stores, diamonds are best cleansed in warm sudsy water with a mild liquid detergent or a little ammonia while scrubbing gently with an eyebrow brush or old toothbrush in the suds. Rinse under warm running water and then dip in rubbing or wood alcohol for fast drying, or place on a tissue to drain."

It's that easy, and what a difference it makes. Keep your diamonds clean and you keep them beautiful. They were meant to be that way. When they're clean, they actually look larger.

While doing household chores, avoid letting your ring or jewelry come in contact with chlorine bleaches, as the mountings may become pitted or discolored. When doing rough work, it is advisable to take the ring off, as a hard blow against a hard object can chip or crack the stone. But *don't* take it off if you are one who forgets where it was put. Almost all insurance men have had loss claims for this reason.

When you are not wearing your jewels, or when traveling, pack them carefully, so they don't touch each other. Diamonds can scratch each other as well as other jewels.

Also, see your jeweler once a year to have your mountings checked for loose stones. A loose diamond may become a lost diamond.

Remember, a diamond is forever and you should get all the pleasure and happiness possible out of the most beautiful of nature's gems.

GLOSSARY

A few words and terms encountered in diamond transactions.

Absolutely Perfect—See "Perfect."

A.G.S.—American Gem Society, professional society whose purpose is to promote gemological education and insure high business standards and ethics.

Appraisal—An evaluation of jewelry for insurance or estate reasons, usually based on replacement value for insurance. Estate valuation is based on quick liquidity in some states, full retail value in others. Inclusion of a photo and exact description of the item is wise procedure in insurance appraisals.

American Cut—See "Ideal Cut."

Baguette—Small rectangular shaped stones, usually used as embellishments in rings or jewelry.

Base—See "Pavilion."

Bearded Girdle—A fuzzy edge due to numerous minute hairlike fractures extending into the stone, giving it a fuzzy appearance.

Bezel facets—The eight large, four-sided facets, the top of which join the table and lower points of the girdle.

Blue-White—A term whose use is discouraged by the Federal Trade Commission and the A.G.S. owing to the flagrant misrepresentation of the term.

Body Color—The color of a diamond when examined under diffused light against a background free from surrounding reflections.

Bombarded Diamond—See "Irradiated Diamond."

Brilliancy—The intensity of the reflections of white light reflected to the eye in the face-up position.

Brilliant cut—Standard round cut. The standard round diamond has fifty-eight facets, thirty-two above the girdle, twenty-four below, the table (the octagonal facet) at the top, and the culet (the smallest facet) at the very bottom of the stone.

Calibre Cut—Very small square, rectangular, or other shape, usually set pavé (for which see entry) as embellishments.

Canary Diamond—An intensely colored yellow diamond, may be slightly orange, but must be deep enough to warrant being termed a "fancy."

Cape—A broad range of color grades covering shades of yellow.

Carat—The term used for weight; 1/142 avoirdupois ounce or 200 milligrams constitutes the metric carat now standard universally.

Carbon Spots—A term used in the jewelry trade; refers to black-appearing inclusions in a diamond.

Certified Gemologist—A title awarded by the American Gem Society to jewelers who have completed special courses in diamonds and colored stones. This field is more comprehensive than that for which the title of Registered Jeweler (see entry) is awarded.

Champagne Color—A greenish yellow to yellow green color, pronounced enough to come under "fancy" classification.

Chip—Usually found in the diamond's edge.

Chip Diamond—A small piece of a crystal or cleavage—used by many to refer to a single cut or very small diamond.

Clarity Grade—The relative position of a diamond on a flawless to imperfect scale.

Clean—A misrepresentative term used by some to denote flawlessness, by others, slight flaws. Frowned on by both the A.G.S. and Federal Trade Commission.

Cleavage Crack—A damaging type of imperfection, often extending to the surface of a diamond. It could affect the durability of the stone.

Cloud—A group of tiny white inclusions that together give a cloudy appearance in the stone.

Color—A basic factor affecting the beauty and value of any diamond. Most diamonds are transparent, with a slight tint, usually yellow or brownish.

Collection Color—A term used by the Diamond Trading Company for finest color grade.

Colorless—A transparent diamond completely devoid of body color, a highly desirable characteristic.

Comparison Stones—Diamonds of known color grades used by some jewelers to determine color grade.

Commercially Clean—A misleading term denoting reasonably free from inclusions or imperfections. Not used by ethical jewelers.

Commercially Perfect—A misleading term to denote "flawlessness. Not used by ethical jewelers.

Crown—The part of a brilliant cut gem above the girdle.

Crystal—An early term still used by a few jewelers. A very slight tinge of yellow is shown in this classification.

Culet—The tiny facet at the very bottom of the diamond.

Cyclotron-Treated Diamond—See Irradiated Diamonds.

Diamond—A mineral composed essentially of pure carbon completely crystallized. The hardest natural substance.

Diamond Cut—Used by some to mean brilliant, or round cut.

Diamond Lamp—Any type of illuminator designed especially for diamond-selling. Beware of blue lamps.

Diamond Loupe—Magnifier for examining the stone. Nothing less than a ten-power corrected lens should be used.

Dispersion—The breaking up of light into colors.

Edge Up—Positioned so stone may be observed parallel to the girdle. Best for detection of any tint of color.

Emerald Cut—A form of step cutting, usually rectangular. If square, it is referred to as square emerald cut.

European Cut—Round diamonds cut with a slightly larger table and slightly different angles compared to "Ideal Cut."

Extra Facet—A facet in excess of the usual planned number. Usually placed in polishing away nicks, chips, naturals, or other faults on or near the surface considered by some as blemishes in grading for cut.

Eye Clean—A term sometimes used (usually misleadingly) to denote no flaws visible to the unaided eye.

Eye Perfect—Same as "Eye Clean." Both terms prohibited by the American Gem Society and the Federal Trade Commission.

Face up—Diamond positioned with the table toward the viewer, the usual position for viewing a mounted stone.

Facet—A plane or polished surface on the diamond.

Fancy—Diamond or "fancy" color. A diamond with a natural, pronounced body color; not off color.

Fancy Cut—Any style other than round.

Finish—The quality of a diamond's polish, the smoothness of its girdle surface, the symmetry of the stone, and the size of the culet.

Fire—Flashes of the different colors of the spectrum as the result of dispersion.

Fisheye—A term used occasionally to refer to a shallow stone devoid of brilliance.

Flaw—Any internal or external imperfection on or in a fashioned diamond.

Flawless—A diamond without blemishes or imperfections. Rare.

Fluorescence—The quality of changing one kind of radiation to another. Under different rays, such as ultraviolet, cathode, or X-ray, the diamond fluoresces a different color, such as blue, and sometimes other colors.

Four C's—Refers to carat (weight), color, clarity (flaws and imperfections), and cut.

Full Cut—In a round diamond, thirty-two facets above, twenty-four below the girdle, the table, and the culet.

Gemologist—A qualified specialist in the knowledge of gems.

G.I.A.—Gemological Institute of America. A nonprofit educational institution, maintained for the benefit of the public and jewelry industry.

Girdle—The extreme outer edge of a fashioned stone.

Grain—The cleavage direction in a diamond.

Hardness—Resistance of material to being scratched. Diamond is the hardest natural material.

Heart Shape—One of the several shapes in which stones are cut.

Ideal Cut—Also called "American cut." Proportions and angles, calculated to obtain maximum brilliancy, devised by mathematician Marcel Tolkowsky. The table is fifty-three percent of the stone's diameter; the depth is 60.3 percent—crown 16.2 percent, pavilion 43.1 percent, and the girdle one percent.

Imperfection—Any internal or external flaw or blemish on a diamond.

Inherent Vice—A characteristic weakness or natural faulty structure in the stone.

Internal Strain—Stress caused by structural irregularities or distortion. A form of inherent vice.

Irradiated Diamond—A diamond bombarded by electrons, neutrons, etc., for the purpose of changing a stone of poor color to an attractive one. See Chapter 15.

Jager—A term sometimes used to designate a stone which has a faint bluish tinge, often caused by strong blue fluorescence.

Loupe—Small magnifying glass. A corrected lens of no less than 10X should be used in examining diamonds.

Luster—The quality of light reflected from the diamond's surface.

Make—A trade term referring to proportions and finish of a diamond.

Marquise—A style of cutting which is boat shaped, pointed at each end. The shape and placement of the facets is similar to the Brilliant cut. Pronounced "Mar-KEYS."

Master Stones—Diamonds of known color grades used as comparison stones to grade other stones for body color.

Mêlée—Small diamonds.

Mohs Hardness Scale—See Chapter 15.

Natural—A term for a portion of the original surface sometimes left by the cutter, usually on the girdle.

Nick—A minor chip out of the surface of a diamond.

Off Color—A diamond having a perceptible tinge of yellow or brown.

Off Round—Cut of round—noticeably unspherical.

Old Mine Cut—An old form of brilliant cutting which has a nearly square girdle.

Open Culet—A larger culet than proper and visible to the naked eye.

Oval Cut—An elliptical outlined shape, faceted in brilliant style.

Pavé—Setting stones closely together to show as little metal as possible.

Pavilion—The lower part of the diamond; the part below the girdle.

Pear Shape—A variation of the brilliant cut, coming to a point at one end, rounded at the other.

Percentage of Imperfection—Such terms as ninety percent perfect or ninety-eight percent perfect, or whatever, are used only by unethical dealers.

Perfect—A flawless stone of fine color and well cut and proportioned. Very rare.

Perfect Cut—So few come under this category that it is considered a misleading term.

Point—One hundredth part of a metric carat.

Polish—See "Luster."

Proportions—The factors which determine cutting quality; proportion of depth to girdle diameter, diameter of table, girdle thickness, facet angles, symmetry, and finish.

Quality—Dependent on cutting, proportions, color grade, and imperfection grade.

Registered Jeweler—A title awarded by the American Gem Society to jewelers whose gemological knowledge has been achieved through special courses and tests based on prescribed course work.

River—An old trade term for color to designate the finest, most transparent colorless diamond.

Scintillation—A flashing or twinkle when the diamond is moved.

Scratches—Marks on a diamond caused by contact with another diamond, or by poor finish.

Slightly Imperfect (S.I.)—Flaws not visible to the unaided eye when facing up.

Swindled Stone—An overspread stone. Cut to save weight at the expense of beauty and brilliancy.

Synthetic Diamond—See Chapter 16.

Synthetic Gem Diamonds—See Chapter 14.

Table—The octagonal facet at the top of a round stone.

Top cape—A yellow cast visible to the unaided eye.

Treated Diamond—See Chapter 15.

V.V.S.I.—Abbreviation for "very, very slight inclusion (or imperfection)."

V.S.I.—Very slight inclusion or imperfection.

Weight—Diamond's weight measured in terms of metric carats.

BIBLIOGRAPHY

Most of the books from which material was gathered are listed here. Other information was obtained from pamphlets, circulars, innumerable issues of trade journals published here and abroad, special reports made for me, and much from personal interviews, letters, and phone calls.

I: Diamonds and the World

Chapter 3—"The Greatest Diamonds of All Time"

Asscher Diamond Works, Amsterdam

Ayer, N. W., and Son, Inc., *Notable Diamonds of the World*, New York, December, 1971.

Balfour, Iain, *Famous Diamonds*, London, February 1968.

Copeland, Lawrence L., *Diamonds, Famous, Notable and Unique*, Los Angeles: Gemological Institute of America, 1966.

Diamond Dictionary, Los Angeles: Gemological Institute of America, 1960.

Historical booklet, Topkapi Museum, Istanbul.

International Diamonds, Johannesburg, 1971.

Kaplan, Lazare, and Sons, New York.

Levinson, Harry, Chicago.

Premier Diamond Mining Co., Pretoria.

Roux, J. E., Information Officer, DeBeers Consolidated Mines, Ltd., London.

Shipley, Robert M., *Famous Diamonds of the World*, Los Angeles: Gemological Institute of America, 1948.

Switzer, Dr. George, "Questing for Gems," *National Geographic*, December 1971.

Tavernier, Jean Baptiste, *My Travels in India* (translated from the original French by H. Milford), London: Oxford University Press, 1925.

"The Growing Desire for Diamonds," *Jewelers Circular-Keystone*, April 1966.

Chapter 4—"Jewels of History"

Ayer, N. W., and Son, Inc., *Notable Diamonds of the World*, New York, December 1971.
Duncan, David Douglas, *Great Treasures of the Kremlin*, New York: Harry N. Abrams, Inc., 1967.
Meen and Tushingham, *Crown Jewels of Iran*, Toronto: University of Toronto Press, 1968.
Ors, Hayrullah, Topkapi Museum, Istanbul.
Twining, Lord, *A History of the Crown Jewels of Europe*, London: B. T. Batsford, Ltd., 1960.

Chapter 5—"The Queen's Necklace"

Carlyle, Thomas, *Critical and Miscellaneous Essays*, Vol. III, London: Chapman.
Castelot, André, *The Queen of France*, New York: Harper and Brothers, 1957.
Dumas, Alexandre, *The Queen's Necklace*, London: Routledge.
Hugo, Victor, *Les Misérables*, Philadelphia: International Press, 1902.
Mossiker, Frances, *The Queen's Necklace*, New York: Simon and Schuster, 1961.

Chapter 7—"Where Diamonds Come From"

Ayer, N. W., and Son, Inc., New York.
Cuddaback, Dr. David, University of California, Berkeley.
Daily, Arthur F.
DeBeers Consolidated Mines, Ltd., London.
"Genesis of Kimberlite," *Diamond Research*, Johannesburg, 1971.

Linholm, Dr. A. A., *Occurrence, Mining and Recovery of Diamonds,* London.
Raal, Dr. F. A., Diamond Research Laboratory, Johannesburg.
U. S. Bureau of Mines, Washington, D. C.

Chapter 8—"A Visit to Kimberley"

Hahn, Emily, *Diamond,* New York: Doubleday, 1957.
"Kimberley 1871–1971," *Diamond News and South African Jeweller,* Special Anniversary Edition, July 1971.
"Kimberley—One Hundred Years," *National Jeweler,* New York, March 1971.
Optima Magazine, Anglo American Corporation, September 1971.

Chapter 9—"Mining: The Search for Needles in a Haystack"

Daily, Arthur F.
International Diamonds, Johannesburg, 1971.
Linholm, Dr. A. A., *Occurrence, Mining and Recovery of Diamonds,* London.
Raal, Dr. F. A. Diamond Research Laboratory, Johannesburg.

Chapter 10—"The Diamond Cutters"

Diamond Dictionary, Los Angeles: Gemological Institute of America, 1960.
Gems and Gemology, Los Angeles: Gemological Institute of America.
International Diamonds, Johannesburg, 1971.
Jooste's Diamond Cutting Works (Pty.) Ltd., Johannesburg.
Ranier, D. M. *Industrial Diamond Review,* London: DeBeers Consolidated Mines, Ltd., 1970.

Roux, J. E., Information Officer, DeBeers Consolidated Mines, Ltd., London.

Tolansky, S., *The Strategic Diamond*, University of London, 1968.

Chapter 11—"From Mine to Milady"

Ayer, N. W., and Son, Inc., New York.

Gemological Institute of America, Los Angeles.

International Diamonds, Johannesburg, 1971.

Chapter 13—"Diamonds U.S.A."

Arkansas Department of Parks, Little Rock.

Ayer, N. W., and Son, Inc., *Notable Diamonds of the World*, New York, December 1971.

California State Library, Sacramento.

Denver Times, March 5, 1899.

Harpending, Asbury, *The Great Diamond Hoax*, University of Oklahoma Press, 1958.

King, Clarence, *Report, Office of Geological Exploration— Fortieth Parallel*, San Francisco, November 11, 1872.

Purtell, Joseph, *The Tiffany Touch*, Random House, 1971.

Rocky Mountain News, Denver, January 27, 1885.

Western Historical Department, Denver Public Library, Denver.

Woodard, Bruce, *Diamonds in the Salt*, Pruett Press, 1967.

Wyoming State Archives and Historical Department, Cheyenne.

Chapter 14—"Synthetic Gem Diamonds"

General Electric Company, Schenectady: Dr. Arthur M. Bueche, Dr. Rodney E. Hanneman, Dr. Herbert Strong, Dr. Robert H. Wentorf

Lindberg, Gene, Denver.

Chapter 15—"Offbeat"

Moed, Irwin, Theodore Moed and Son, New York.
South African Mining and Engineering Journal, December 1961.
Gemological Institute of America, pamphlets, Los Angeles.
Jewelers Circular-Keystone, Philadelphia, May 1971.

Chapter 16—"Diamonds at Work"

Diamond Research Laboratory, Johannesburg.
Industrial Diamond Review, London.
Lindberg, Gene, Denver.
Silveri, Peter and Associates, New York.

II: Diamonds and You

Chapter 7—"Investment"

"Behind the Grit and the Glitter," *Forbes Magazine,* February 1970.
"Diamonds vs. Blue Chips," *New York Times Sunday Magazine,* April 14, 1962.
McDonald, John, "Diamonds for the Masses," *Fortune Magazine,* December 1964.

Chapter 8—"Insurance"
National Jeweler, New York.
Thomas, Cosby, Denver.

"Glossary"

Diamond Dictionary, Gemological Institute of America, Los Angeles, 1960.

Acknowledgments

In addition to those listed at the front of the book, I thank each of the following individuals and publications for assistance and cooperation in my project:

Robert Anholt, Yehuda Appelberg, Ed Armes, Louis Asscher, Iain Balfour, Eisik Bar, Susan Boatright, Lionel Burke, Charles F. Buxton, Helen Fletcher Collins, A. F. Daily, *Diamond News and South African Jeweller*, R. A. Dickson, Mrs. F. William Freeze, Allen Ginsberg, Barbara Gleason, Frances Gordon, Michael Grantham, Dr. Rodney Hanneman, William Hornby, *Industrial Diamond Review*, Betsey Irwin, Lazare Kaplan and Sons, Mildred Kosick, R. Ned Langdon, W. J. Lear, Edward Littlehales, A. Markiewicz, Florence McDermott, Vincent McMorrow, Eunice Miles, Leslie Mirin, Irwin Moed, Dr. Frederick Pough, Mary Louise Riede, Gerald Rothschild, Peter Silveri, Irving Sherman, His Excellency Arnold Smith, Professor Carlyle Smith, H. Wallace Steinmetz, Herbert Stoenner, Cosby Thomas, R. K. Timothy, Amy Vanderbilt, Howard Vaughan, Anita Viksne, Colonel George Visser, Harry Wheeler.

Index

Abdul Hamid II, Sultan, 30, 31, 57;
  illus., 56
Adkins, Homer, 181
Aga Khan, 23–25; *illus.*, 24
Ahmed Pasha, Grand Vizier, 59
Ahmed Shah, 36
Alexander III, King of Scotland, 63
Ali Pasha, 59
Alluvial diamonds, 107–8, 131, 171
American cut, 245, 273; *illus.*, 245
American Diamond Jewelry Competi-
  tion, 168–69, 224
American Gem Society, 250, 269
Amsterdam, Netherlands, 145
Anderson, B. W., 198
Angola, diamonds in, 102–3
Antwerp, Belgium, 145
Appraisal, 257, 266, 269
Arc diamond, 73
Argenzio, Victor, 213–24
Arkansas, diamonds in, 6, 181–83
Arkansas Crystal, 183
Arkansas (Searcy) diamond, 183
Arnold, Philip, 184–88
A.S.E.A., 204
Ashberg diamond, 77
Asscher, Joseph, 42, 222
Asscher, Louis, 42, 222
Asscher Brothers, 41–42
Atherstone, Dr. W., 100
Aurangzeb, Emperor, 17, 153
Aurelian, Emperor, 62
Ayer (N. W.) and Son, Inc., 168

Baber, Emperor, 33–34
Baguette diamonds, 269; *illus.*, 243
Baken Diamante, 107
Balfour, Iain, 39
Bar Sur Aube, Bishop of, 81
Bargains, 255–56
Barge 77, 110, 136; *illus.*, 109
Barion cut, 144–45
Barlow, Samuel, 187, 188
Barnato, Barney, 123–27; *illus.*, 124

Baumgold Brothers, 75
Baumgold Rough diamond, 72
Baumgold II diamond, 73
Baxter-Brown, R., 107
Bearded girdle, 236, 247, 269
Berglen diamond, 73
Bessenger (French court jeweler), 78,
  83
Betrothal, 21
Bezel facets, 269
Big Hole, Kimberley mine, 119; *illus.*,
  102, 118
Birmingham diamond, 183
Black spots, removal of, 198–99
Black Star of Africa, 76
Block caving, 134
Blockers, 150
Blue Diamond of the Crown, 30, 45.
  See also Hope diamond
Blue ground, 133
Blue-White, 251, 269
Boat-shaped. See Marquise cut
Body color, 269
Böhmer (French court jeweler), 78, 80,
  83
Book of Diamonds (Dickenson), 31
Borgio, Hortensio, 153
Bort, 22, 203
Botha, Louis, 41
Botswana, diamonds in, 105
Boulainvilliers, Marquise de, 81
Bowes, Major, 197
Brady, Diamond Jim, 25–26, 85,
  209–10; *illus.*, 25
Brazil, diamonds in, 99–100, 106,
  130–31
Brilliancy, 269
Brilliant cut, 143, 239, 241–44, 246, 269;
  illus., 240
Brillianteering, 152, 241
Broderick diamond, 73
Brokers, 154–56
Bruting, 149–50
Bruton, Eric, 223

Bubbles, 235
Bueche, Dr. Arthur M., 189, 191, 223
Bulgari, Paolo, 7
Bultfontein mine, 101
Burton, Richard, 3
Butler, General Benjamin F., 187
Buying diamonds, 227–29, 253–58

Calibre cut, 270
Canadian-South African Diamond
  Corporation, Ltd., 107–8
Canary diamond, 270
Cape, 270
Carat, 9, 230–33, 270
Carbon spots, 235, 270; removal of,
  198–99
Care of diamonds, 267–68
Carlyle, Thomas, 80
Carraway, Hattie, 181
Cartier, Pierre, 30
Cartier's, 3
Casanova, 59
Casanova lottery diamond, 59, 69
Case 007, 174–76
Castelo Branco, Humberto, President
  of Brazil, 176
Castelot, André, 80
Catherine II, Empress of Russia,
  49–50; illus., 48
Cellini, Benvenuto, 141
Cent Six diamond, 77
Center for Short-Lived Phenomena,
  94
Center stone, 233
Champagne color, 270
Chandler, Arizona, 146
Charlemagne, King of the Franks, 15,
  209; illus., 14
Charles II, King of Scotland, 63
Charles V, Holy Roman Emperor, 209
Charles VII, King of France, 20
Charles X, King of France, 45–46
Chief of Carlisle diamond, 183
Chip (flaw), 236, 270
Chip diamond, 270
Clarity, 234–38
Clarity grade, 270
Classification, 237–38
Clean, 270
Cleavage crack, 236, 270
Cleaving, 146–48. See also Cutting
Clouds, 236, 270
Clubs, diamond, 11, 159, 160–63
Coastal diamonds, 111–13
Cohen, Julius, 75
Collection color, 271

Collins, Sam, 109–11, 136
Color, 249–52, 270; changes in, 196–98;
  measurement of, 250–51
Colorlessness, 249, 271
Commercial White, 251
Commercially clean, 271
Commercially perfect, 271
Compagnie Française de Diamant,
  125–26
Comparison stones, 271
Congo, Republic of the, diamonds in,
  102, 116
Consolidated Diamond Mines of
  South West Africa, Ltd., 111, 134–36
Constantine, Emperor, 62
Coromandel diamond, 73
Corundum, 195
Cotton Belt Star, 183
Crater of Diamonds, Arkansas, 181–83;
  illus., 180
Cross of Asia diamond, 77
Crown, 241, 271; illus., 242
Crown jewels: of Great Britain, 37, 43,
  60–61; illus., 60, 61, 63; of Iran, 62,
  65–66; of Russia, 65; illus., 64, 65, 66;
  of Scotland, 62–64; illus., 64
Crowningshield, Robert, 164, 198
Crystal, 251, 271
Crystalline form, 5
Culet, 143, 152, 241, 244, 271; open, 274
Cullinan, Sir Thomas, 41, 101–2
Cullinan diamond, 39–43, 62, 117, 222;
  cutting, 41–42, 71–72, 148; illus., 40,
  71; weight, 9, 71
Cullinan I, 43, 74, 99; illus., 40
Cullinan II, 43, 74
Cullinan III, 43; illus., 63
Cullinan IV, 43; illus., 63
Cuts, of diamonds, 239–48. See also
  names of specific cuts
Cutters, 247
Cutting, 141–53; of the Cullinan, 41–42,
  71–72, 148; of the Jonker, 52–54, 148;
  of the Light of Peace, 91–92; loss in,
  71–72, 240
Cyrus the Great, 39

Darcy Vargas diamond, 73
Darya-i-Nur, 37–39, 74, 76
Dating, of diamonds, 95–96
de Berquem, Louis, 141–42
Dealers, diamond, 11–12, 160–63
DeBeer, Diedrich Arnoldus, 123
DeBeer, Joannes Nicholas, 123
DeBeers Consolidated Mines, Ltd.,
  101, 105, 110, 116, 126–28, 168, 262

DeBeers diamond, 73, 76
DeBeers Research Laboratory, 138
Deepdene diamond, 77, 198
Dewey diamond, 183
Diamond, 271. *See also* Gem diamonds; Industrial diamonds; Synthetic diamonds; names of specific diamonds
Diamond Ball, 91, 168
Diamond clubs, 11, 159, 160–63
Diamond Corporation, 52
Diamond cut, 271
Diamond lamp, 271
Diamond Research Laboratory, 113
Diamond Street, New York, N.Y., 11, 12
Diamond trade, illegal, 170–72, 173–76, 179
Diamond Trading Company, 154, 155–60
Diamondlite, 250
Diamonds-International Academy, 168
Diamonds-International Awards, 165–69
Diario Minas Gerais, 73
Dickenson, Jean, 31
Diggers' Rest (bar), 120
Distribution, 11, 154–64
Dops, 148, 149
Dorset, Duke of, 85
Dowagiac diamond, 183
Drills, diamond, 202, 203, 207–8
Drukker, D. (firm), 22
Du Barry, Madame, 78–79
Dutoitspan mine, 101
Dyortsville diamond, 183

Eagle diamond, 183
Earth Star, 75
East India Company, 36, 56
Edge up, 271
Edison, Thomas, 10
Edward VII, King of England, 41
Elizabeth, Queen Mother, 37
Elizabeth II, Queen of England, 103, 117; *illus.*, 61
Emerald cut, 143, 197, 239, 245–46, 271; *illus.*, 240
Engagé, 217–18
Engagement rings, 6, 8, 12
Eugénie, Empress, 46
Eureka diamond, 100
European cut, 245, 271
Evener, Marion Dell, 182
Excelsior diamond, 41, 71, 72

Extra facets, 236, 247, 271
Eye clean, 272
Eye perfect, 237–38, 272

Face up, 272
Facet, 241, 272; bezel, 269; extra, 236, 247, 271
Faceting, 150, 241
Fancy, 272
Fancy cut, 272
Farah, Empress, 39
Farouk I, King of Egypt, 54, 77
Fath Ali, 38
Feathers, 236
Federal Trade Commission (FTC), 197, 199, 237, 251, 257
Fences, 179
Fields, Leo, 86
Fincham, Allister, 104–5, 114
Fine White, 251
Finest White, 251
Finish, 241, 272
Finsch mine, 104–5; *illus.*, 104
Fire, 272
Fisheye, 272
Flaw, 235–38, 272
Flawless, 272
Florentine diamond, 76
Fluorescence, 272
Ford, Henry, 181
Francis I, King of France, 209
Francis II, Emperor of Austria, 45
French Coral diamond, 183
Full cut, 150, 241–43, 272

Garnets: pyrope, 104, 114; yttrium aluminum, 195
Garry Moore diamond, 183
Gem diamonds, 11; cut, 74–77; rough, 72–73, 140, 183; synthetic, 189–93, 262; in the U.S., 183. *See also* names of specific diamonds
Gemological Insitute of America (G.I.A.), 164–65, 198, 217, 250, 272
Gemologists, 270; certified, 271
Gemology, 164–65
General Electric Company, 189–93, 204
Genghis Khan, 15
Geology, of diamonds, 94–98
George III, King of England, 77
George IV, King of England, 63
Ghana, diamonds in, 103, 105
Giannini, A. P., 215–16
Ginsberg, Allen, 88

Girdle, 142, 241, 272; bearded, 236, 247, 269; coloring of, 196; *illus.*, 242
Girdling, 149–50
Golconda fields, India, 15, 38, 55, 98
Goudvis Company, 22–23
Goyaz diamond, 72
Grain, 273
Graphite, 5
Grease tables, 133–34
Great Brazilian diamond, 76
Great Chrysanthemum diamond, 75
Great Mogul diamond, 50, 72, 76, 158
Great Star of Africa, *illus.*, 60
Great Table, 38. *See also* Darya-i-Nur
Green, Robert L., 168
Grinding, 143
Guarantees, 256
Gübelin, Dr. Edward, 198
Guinea, diamonds in, 105
Gulistan Palace, Teheran, 18
Guyand, diamonds in, 107
Gwalior, Rajah of, 33

Hannay, J. R., 204
Hardness, 273; of diamond, 195, 200, 229; Mohs scale of, 195
Hastings diamond, 77
Heart-shaped, 143, 240, 273; *illus.*, 240
Heat conductivity, in diamonds, 207
Henry VIII, King of England, 209
Hoaxes, 184–88
Hong Kong, sale of diamonds in, 6
Hope, Henry Francis Hope Pelham-Clinton-, 30, 31
Hope, Henry Philip, 30
Hope, Sir Henry Thomas, 30
Hope diamond, 18, 28–33, 69, 130; *illus.*, 29
Hotel Pierre, New York, N.Y., 177
Houthaker (South African digger), 21–22
Hoving, Walter, 212
How King of Diamonds Was Trumped (Robb), 178–79
Howard, Mrs. P., 181–82
Humayun, Emperor, 33

Ice Queen diamond, 73
Ideal cut, 245, 273; *illus.*, 245
Identification, 229
Idol's Eye, 30, 54–58, 264; *illus.*, 55
Imitation diamonds, 194–96. *See also* Synthetic diamonds
Imperfections, 235–38, 273
India: cutting in, 146; diamonds in, 98–99, 130. *See also* Golconda fields

Indien diamond, 176
Industrial diamonds, 10–11, 200–8; synthetic, 189, 200, 204–5
Inherent vice, 265, 273
Institute of International Education, 91, 168
Insurance, 265–66
Internal strain, 273
International Congress of Weights and Measures, 230
International Diamond Security Organization, 172
Investing, 259–64
Iranian A diamond, 74
Iranian B diamond, 74
Iranian C diamond, 75
Iranian D diamond, 75
Iranian E diamond, 75
Irradiation, 196–98, 273
Isaacs, Barnett. *See* Barnato, Barney
Isaacs, Harry, 123
Israel: cutting in, 145; merchandising in, 161–62
Ivory Coast, diamonds in, 105

Jacob diamond, 77
Jacobs (Boer farmer), 100
Jager, 273
Jagersfontein mine, 101, 105, 131
Janin, Henry, 184
Japan, diamond sales in, 6, 260
Jehangir, Emperor, 15
Jenner-Clarke, H., 107
Jewelers: registered, 274; retail, 163–64, 254–55
Johnson, Mrs. Lyndon B., 92, 93
Jones, Harford, 38
Jonker, Jacobus, 50–52
Jonker diamond, 50–54, 72, 75, 148; *illus.*, 51
Jooste's Cutting Works, 145
Jubilee diamond, 74
Julius Pam diamond, 76

Kaplan, Lazare, 52–54; *illus.*, 53
Kaplan, Leo, 53
Kaplan, Peter, 54
Kaplan (Lazare) and Sons, 191
Kashmir, Sheik of, 57
Kasicki diamond, 58–59, 69; *illus.*, 58
Keeble, Peter, 108–11, 136
"Kelly, Father," 177
Khojeh (Persian merchant), 49
Kimberley Central Mining, 126, 127
Kimberley Club, 117, 127

Kimberley mine, 101, 105, 107, 116–29, 131
Kimberlite pipes, 94, 97, 105
King, Clarence, 188
Kirsten (engineer), 133
Kohinoor diamond, 28, 33–37, 38, 56, 62, 69, 75, 130; *illus.*, 34, 36
Kublai Khan, 15

La Motte, Jeanne, Countess de, 80–85
La Motte, Marc Antoine, Count de, 81–84
La Porte (French lawyer), 80, 81
Lasers, and spot removal, 198–99
Lee diamond, 183
Lesotho, diamonds in, 105–6
Lesotho diamond, 72; *illus.*, 106
Lesotho B diamond, 72
Levinson, Harry, 58
Liberia, smuggling in, 170–72
Liddicoat, Richard T., 164
Light dispersion, 241, 271
Light of Peace, 11, 73, 74, 86–93; *illus.*, 87, 90
Lipshy, Ben, 89
Liquidity, of diamonds, 264
Louis XIV, King of France, 18, 29–30, 31
Louis XV, King of France, 45, 78, 79
Louis XVI, King of France, 18–19, 31, 45, 62; and Queen's Necklace affair, 78, 79, 80, 81
Louis XVII, King of France, 78
Louis XVIII, King of France, 45
Loupe, 234, 271, 273
Luster, 273

McClellan, General George B., 187, 188
McGill, Dr. William, 92
McHardy, William, 40
McLean, Edward B., 30, 31–32
McLean, Evalyn Walsh, 30–31, 32
Mahmut II, Sultan, 59
Mail-order diamonds, 255
Make, 241, 273
Malwa, Rajah of, 33
Man-made diamonds, 191, 192
Maria Theresa, Empress, 82
Marie Antoinette, Queen of France, 19, 31, 45; and Queen's Necklace affair, 78–85
Marie Louise, Empress, 19, 45
Marketing, 154–64
Markham, Ronald V., 108

Marquise cut, 143, 197, 240, 246, 273; *illus.*, 240
Martin, Glenn, 181
Marx, Harpo, 25
Mary of Burgundy, 21
Master stones, 273
Maximilian I, Holy Roman Emperor, 21
May, Mrs. Herbert, 19
"*Mazel und broche*," 11–12, 163
Means, Gaston, 32
Measurement of diamonds, 9–10. *See also* Weight
Mehmed IV, Sultan, 59
Meister, Walter, 75
Meister diamond, 75
Mêlée, 273
Men, diamonds for, 209–12
Meteorite diamonds, 94
Milford diamond, 183
Minas Gerais, Brazil, 99, 100
Mines: development of, 116–29; security in, 172, 173. *See also* names of specific mines
Mining techniques, 130–39
Mirabeau, Count de, 85
Mohammed Reza Shah Pahlavi, 39, 66
Mohammed Shah, 35
Mohs scale of hardness, 195
Moissan, Henri, 204
Monopoly, of diamond industry, 128–29
Moon diamond, 76
Moon of Mountains, 76
Morgantown diamond, 183
Morrow diamond, 183
Mounce diamond, 183
Mountain of Splendor, 76
Mumtaz Mahal, 34
Murfreesboro, Arkansas, 6, 181–83

Nadir Shah, 18, 35, 38, 50, 66
Napoleon I, Emperor, 19, 45, 59, 85
Napoleon III, Emperor, 46
Nasser ed-din-Shah, 39
Naturals, 236, 273
Nawanger diamond, 74
Nepal, Queen of, 54
New York, New York: diamond business in, 11, 12, 160, 162–63; diamond thefts in, 176–77, 178–79
Newmann, Vera, 168
Niarchos, Stavros P., 74
Niarchos diamond, 74
Nicks, 236, 274
Nizam diamond, 74

North light, 251
Nur ul-ain diamond, 38–39

Off color, 274
Off round, 274
Offshore diamond deposits, 108–11
Old Mine cut, 274
Open culet, 274
Oppenheimer, Sir Ernest, 22, 128
Oppenheimer, Harry, 128
Orapa pipe, 105
O'Reilly, Mr., 100
Orloff, Gregory, Prince, 49–50
Orloff diamond, 46–50, 69, 74, 130;
    illus., 47, 49
Oval cut, 143, 239, 246, 274; *illus.*, 240

Pahlavi Crown, 66; *illus.*, 67
Parker, Mrs. Arthur, 181
Pavé, 270, 274
Pavilion, 241, 274
Peacock Throne, 17–18, *illus.*, 17, 18
Pear-shaped, 143, 197, 239, 246, 274;
    illus., 240
Peiken Jewelers, 181
Pendeloque. *See* Pear-shaped
Percentage of imperfection, 238, 274
Perfect cut, 247–48, 274
Perfect diamond, 236–37, 257, 274
Peruzzi, Vincenti, 143
Peterstown, West Virginia, 181
Philippe II, Duke of Orléans, 45
Phonograph needles, 206–7
Pike County, Arkansas, 6, 181–83
Pikot (French officer), 59
Pikot diamond, 59, 69
Pitau, Sieur, 30
Pitt, Thomas, 43–45
Pitt diamond, 45, 73. *See also* Regent
    diamond
Planners, 146
Pliny the Elder, 13
Point, 9–10, 230, 274
Polishing, 152, 241
Polo, Marco, 15
Popugaieva, Larissa, 114
Portuguese diamond, 75
Pough, Dr. Frederick, 197
Premier Diamond Mining Company,
    Ltd., 41
Premier mine, 39–40, 96, 101–2, 103,
    116–17; *illus.*, 102
Presidente Dutra diamond, 73
Presidente Vargas diamond, 52, 72
Prices, 261–62
Prinsloo, Joachim, 101

Production, 98–116
Proportions, 274
Punch Jones diamond, 181, 183
Purchasing diamonds, 227–29, 253–58
Pyrope garnets, 104, 114

Quality, 274
Quartz, hardness of, 195
Queen of France (Castelot), 80
Queen of Holland diamond, 76
Queen's Necklace affair, 78–85; *illus.*,
    79

Ramaboa, Ernestine, 105–6
Ramaboa, Petrus, 106
Ramchund (Indian merchant), 43
Ramolino, Letizia, 59
Ranjit Singh, 36
Rasheetah, Princess, 57
Rasid (Ottoman historian), 58–59
Raulconda diamond, 77
Rawstone, Fleetwood, 119–20
Red Cross diamond, 73, 76
Red diamond, 21–23
Refractometer, 229
Regent diamond, 43–46, 73, 74; *illus.*,
    44, 46
Rehab (Persian prince), 56
Reitz diamond, 72
Rhodes, Cecil John, 121–23, 125–27,
    131; *illus.*, 122
Rhodes, Herbert, 122
River, 251, 274
Robb, Inez, 178
Robbery. *See* Thefts
Rohan, Louis-René-Éduard, Cardi-
    nal, 81–85
Rojtman, Mrs. Marc, 75
Rojtman diamond, 75
Roosevelt, Franklin D., 181
Round cut, 197, 239, 241–44, 246, 269;
    illus., 240
Rounding, 149–50, 241
Ruby, hardness of, 195
Russell, Lillian, 26, 85
Russia. *See* Soviet Russia

San Francisco and New York Mining
    and Commercial Company, 184
Sandilands, J., 117
Sapphires, 195
Saukville diamond, 183
Sawing, 143, 148–49, 241. *See also*
    Cutting
Scaif, 150
Schiffmann, Charles A., 197

Scintillation, 254, 275
Scott, Sir Walter, 63
Scratches, 275
Sea mining, 108–11, 136–37
Searcy diamond, 183
Shah Jehan, 15, 34; *illus.*, 16
Shah Rukh, 35
Shah Shuja, 36
Shaping, 149–50
Shipley, Robert M., 42, 164
S.I., 237, 275
Sierra Leone, diamonds in, 88, 103; diamond thefts in, 170–72
Sierra Leone Selection Trust, Ltd., 170–71
Sights, 156–57
Single cut, 142, 150, 243–44; *illus.*, 243
Slack, John, 184–88
Slightly imperfect, 237, 275
Smith, Carlyle H., 212
Smithsonian Institution, Washington, D.C., 19, 31, 33, 183, 191
Smuggling, 170–72
Sorel, Agnès, 20
South Africa: diamonds in, 100–2, 103–5; mining in, 5, 117–29, 131
South Africa Company, 127
Southwest Africa, diamonds in, 102
Soviet Russia: diamonds in, 114–15; mining techniques in, 5, 137–38; smuggling in, 170
Spectroscope, 229
Spinel, synthetic, 195
Spoon Maker diamond, 58–59, 69; *illus.*, 58
Square cut, 143
Square emerald cut, 143, 271
Stanley diamond, 183
Stanton, May Bonfils, 57
Star of Arkansas, 181, 183
Star of Diamonds, 77
Star of Egypt, 77
Star of Sierra Leone, 70, 71, 72, 103; *illus.*, 70
Star of the East, 77
Star of the South, 74
Step cut, 143–44
Stewart diamond, 77
Strong, Dr. Herbert M., 189–90, 191
Strontium titanate, 195
Stumpo, Luigi, 10
Superstition, and the Hope diamond, 31–33
Sutherland, Dutchess of, 85
Swindled stones, 245, 275
Switch artists, 177, 178–79

Switzer, Dr. George, 33
Synthetic diamonds, 96; gem, 189–93, 262; industrial, 189, 200, 204–5. *See also* Imitation diamonds

Table, 142, 241, 275
Taj-E-Mah diamond, 38, 75
Talc, hardness of, 195
Tallyrand, Charles, 85
Tanzania, diamonds in, 103
Tavernier, Jean Baptiste, 15–18, 28–29, 38, 50, 130; *illus.*, 16
Taylor, Elizabeth, 3
Taylor-Burton diamond, *illus.*, 3
Teheran, Iran, 18
Thefts, 45, 170–72, 173, 176–79
Theresa diamond, 183
Thomson, Lord, 223
Tiffany, Chalres, 187
Tiffany and Company, 23, 25, 178, 182, 187, 212
Tiffany diamond, 74
Timur, 36
Tolkowsky, Marcel, 143, 273
Top cape, 275
Top Crystal, 251
Top Wesselton, 251
Topaz, hardness of, 195
Topkapi Museum, Istanbul, Turkey, 58, 67–69
Turkey I diamond, 76
IIa industrial diamond, 207

Uncle Sam diamond, 181, 183
United States: cutting in, 145–46; diamond sales in, 6, 7; diamonds in, 5–6, 180–83

Vacuveyor, *illus.*, 136
Van Berken, Lodewyk, 141–42
Van Niekirk, Mr., 100–1
Vanderbilt, Amy, 267–68
Venezuela, diamonds in, 106–7
Venter diamond, 73
Victoria, Queen of England, 36–37
Victoria 1880 diamond, 73, 76
Victoria 1884 diamond, 73, 76
Villette, Marc Antoine Rétaux de, 82, 83, 84
Visser, Colonel George, 220
Voorsanger (Dutch cutter), 36
V.S.I., 237, 275
V.V.S.I., 237, 275

Watermeyer, Basil, 144
Weight, 9–10, 230–33, 275

Weiller, Paul-Louis, 74
Wells, Frederick, 39–40
Wentorf, Dr. Robert H., 189–90, 191
Wesselton, 251
Wesselton mine, 101
Wholesale diamonds, 255
Williamson, Dr. John T., 103
Windows, 146
Winston, Edna, 32–33
Winston, Harry, 31, 32–33, 52, 54, 57, 70, 178–79
Winston diamond-cutting plant, 146
Winston (Harry), Inc., 178
Wire drawing, 202
Woyie River diamond, 72, 103

X-ray luminescence, 138
X-ray separation technique, 137–38

Yttrium aluminum garnet (YAG), 195

Zaire, diamonds in, 102, 116
Zale, Donald, 92
Zale, Morris B., 89, 91
Zale Award Committee, 92–93
Zale Corporation, 86
Zale Foundation, 92
Zand, Lutf Ali Khan, 38
Zeman, 36
Zenobia, Queen of Palmyra, 13–14
Zvi, Ben, 92